SEASONS OF MY LIFE

6

SEASONS
OF MY LIFE
Tales from a solitary Daleswoman

Hannah Hauxwell

with Barry Cockcroft

An Orion paperback

First published in Great Britain in 1989
by Century Hutchinson Ltd
This paperback edition published in 2012
by Orion Books Ltd,
Orion House, 5 Upper St Martin's Lane,
London WC2H 9EA

An Hachette UK company

1 3 5 7 9 10 8 6 4 2

A CIP catalogue record for this book is available
from the British Library.

ISBN 978-1-4091-3623-1

Typeset at the Spartan Press Ltd,
Lymington, Hants

Printed and bound in Great Britain by CPI Group (UK) Ltd,
Croydon, CRO 4YY

The Orion Publishing Group's policy is to use papers that
are natural, renewable and recyclable products and
made from wood grown in sustainable forests. The logging
and manufacturing processes are expected to conform to
the environmental regulations of the country of origin.

www.orionbooks.co.uk

CONTENTS

Preface 1

Introduction 9

1 Baldersdale – A Classic Yorkshire Dale 15

2 Portrait of an Enclosed Community 25

3 'Too Long a Winter' 51

A Bird's-eye View of Baldersdale 58

4 Dreams of Romance 73

5 My Music . . . the Talented Tallentires
and a Poetic Grandad 83

6 Festive Times . . . and Funerals 91

7 My Friends, the Beasts of the Field 111

8 Housekeeping . . . and Health 125

9 Travel . . . from Tommy's Bus to the Savoy
and Buckingham Palace 133

10 The True Daughter of Balder . . . from
Another Point of View 149

11 The 'Heirs' of Hannah 175

Postscript 183

Acknowledgement 195

LIST OF ILLUSTRATIONS

First section

Grandmother Hauxwell and Uncle Thomas
Buttermaking at Cotherstone (Beamish, North of
    England Open Air Museum)
Sweeping hay (Beamish, North of England Open Air
    Museum)
Hury Show (Beamish, North of England Open Air
    Museum)
Sheep shearing
Sheep dipping
Grandfather James and Grandmother Hauxwell
Sam Fawcett
Hannah's mother as a young woman
Hannah as a teenager
Haytime (Beamish, North of England Open Air
    Museum)
Baldersdale school
John Thwaites
Hannah (Press Association)

Second section

Hannah and Barry Cockcroft
Hannah with friends
Hannah and her belongings
Hannah asleep
Hannah's kitchen window
Winter in Baldersdale
Feeding cattle
At the door of Low Birk Hatt
Hannah
Low Birk Hatt
Hannah and Timmy
Hannah with Ashley Jackson
View of Low Birk Hatt

(All photographs in this section were taken by Mostafa
  Hammuri)

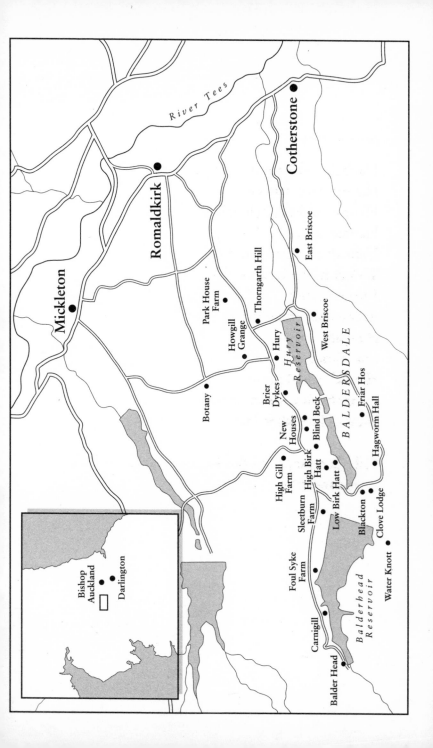

PREFACE

As she speaks, the cadences are clearly rooted in another time . . . a more mannered time. Late eighteenth or early nineteenth century perhaps. One thing is certain, however: when Hannah Hauxwell speaks, people listen. She possesses a quality which cannot properly be defined.

She talks guilelessly about her abiding love for her surroundings. Low Birk Hatt Farm lies in the desolate and partially abandoned sweep of Baldersdale, high in the Pennines. It is frequently uncomfortable in summer and a bleak prison sentence in winter. But to Hannah, whatever the physical discomforts, it is an enchanted land.

She puts her feelings into words, a strangely compelling, rhythmic web of sentences, and her listeners are obviously captivated. Hard-bitten and unsentimental they are, too, like all much-travelled and over-privileged film crews. But their highly polished veneer of cynicism dissolves under the wash of a curious tide of articulate innocence.

*

It's my favourite place, here . . . down the new road through the iron gate. I stand here and watch the seasons come and go. At night the moonlight plays on Hunder Beck . . . and the waters sing a song to me . . .

I know this place will always be loyal to me. If I have nothing in my pocket I will always have this. They cannot take it away from me. It's mine, mine for the taking, and always will be . . . even when I'm no longer here.

A significant pause, and Hannah looks away over the glistening waters. When she turns back her eyes are flooding with tears. The film crew is stilled, like a freeze frame. Hannah recovers, smiles tremulously and concludes . . .

Of course, I suppose I shall have to leave here . . . sooner rather than later, I imagine. It will not be an easy thing to do.

But in years to come, if you see a ghost walking here you can be sure it will be me.

Hannah falls silent, and smiles again. Slowly, the film crew emerge from their trance. Those who know her never fail to wonder at the remarkable effect she has on people, however grand, whatever their background.

Of course, Hannah loves to talk because she rarely has the opportunity of conversation, of engaging an audience. She lives alone, a true castaway of life . . . trapped by circumstances in the sepia squalor of Low Birk Hatt.

She has the animals, her only constant companions. Her family, she calls them . . . and they are outrageously indulged, from the undisciplined dog through to the irritable old cow. They all have names and she talks to them as though they are human. As conversations go they are a trifle one-sided, but nine days out of ten they are all she has. Low Birk Hatt must be the loneliest place in the Kingdom. They are so special to her, these dumb and clumsy beasts, that she can talk sorrowfully about some which departed for the glue factory decades ago.

Oh, and can she talk, this simple, ragged lady of the high Pennines. The words are soft and gentle but they can penetrate the soul. Which other ordinary, workaday person, someone who has achieved nothing in life by the standards laid down by society, has had two enormously successful, internationally networked film documentaries made about her, and is even now in the process of making a *third*?

She has left her isolation just twice in her sixty-two

years – once to be a guest of honour at the 'Women of the Year' lunch at the Savoy Hotel (where she was besieged by Press and celebrities, including the wife of the then Prime Minister, plus minor royalty) and once to attend a Buckingham Palace garden party.

The third film may create the biggest impact of all. For this time she is going to leave Low Birk Hatt permanently . . . has to. If she stops the process she has so reluctantly started – the valuation of her land and cattle, the perusal of cottages for sale in the nearby villages – then the likely consequences do not bear contemplation . . . to be found dead, one killing winter, lying on the frozen stone slabs of her kitchen floor, partly eaten by rats.

Whatever happens, any television programme about Hannah will generate a great deal of emotion. She has countless devotees, who flood her farm with letters and presents and create serious space problems.

In the meantime, she talks . . . fascinatingly, poetically, about the seasons of her life. Her childhood . . . chapel . . . the horses that once worked the farm . . . the birds and wildlife . . . the changes wrought by the seasons . . . grandparents, uncles and aunts . . . the loneliness and hardships after all her relatives die . . . music and poetry appreciation as taught by her mother.

Here are all the reference points of life through

the eyes and emotions of Hannah Bayles Tallentire
Hauxwell . . . the lady with the inspirational quality
which defies analysis.

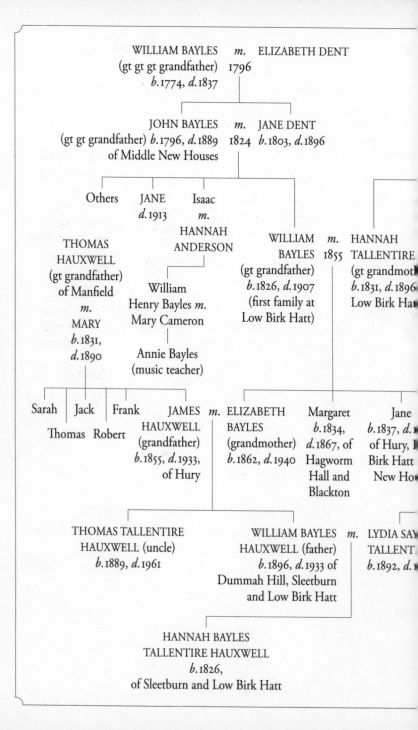

WILLIAM BAYLES   m.   ELIZABETH DENT
(gt gt gt grandfather)   1796
b.1774, d.1837

JOHN BAYLES   m.   JANE DENT
(gt gt grandfather) b.1796, d.1889   1824   b.1803, d.1896
of Middle New Houses

Others   JANE   Isaac
d.1913   m.

THOMAS   HANNAH
HAUXWELL   ANDERSON   WILLIAM   m.   HANNAH
(gt grandfather)   BAYLES   1855   TALLENTIRE
of Manfield   William   (gt grandfather)   (gt grandmot|
m.   Henry Bayles m.   b.1826, d.1907   b.1831, d.1896
MARY   Mary Cameron   (first family at   Low Birk Ha|
b.1831,   Low Birk Hatt)
d.1890   Annie Bayles
(music teacher)

Sarah   Jack   Frank   JAMES   m.   ELIZABETH   Margaret   Jane
    HAUXWELL   BAYLES   b.1834,   b.1837, d.|
Thomas   Robert   (grandfather)   (grandmother)   d.1867, of   of Hury, |
    b.1855, d.1933,   b.1862, d.1940   Hagworm   Birk Hatt
    of Hury   Hall and   New Ho|
    Blackton

THOMAS TALLENTIRE   WILLIAM BAYLES   m.   LYDIA SA|
HAUXWELL (uncle)   HAUXWELL (father)   TALLENT.
b.1889, d.1961   b.1896, d.1933 of   b.1892, d.|
    Dummah Hill, Sleetburn
    and Low Birk Hatt

HANNAH BAYLES
TALLENTIRE HAUXWELL
b.1826,
of Sleetburn and Low Birk Hatt

HANNAH BAYLES TALLENTIRE HAUXWELL
FAMILY TREE

◆

ISAAC TALLENTIRE   *m.*   ELIZABETH (BETTY)
(gt gt grandfather)   (gt gt grandmother)
of Pike Stone, Holwick

MARK SAYER
(gt grandfather)
m.
WALTON
(gt grandmother) of
Manor House Farm
and Temperance
Hotel, Bowes

aac 823, 892	Margaret	Richard of Sleetburn and Low Fields S. Stainmore	Thomas *b.*1826, *d.*1903	WILLIAM TALLENTIRE (gt grandfather) *m.* LEE (gt grandmother)

es	John	Isaac *b.*1852, *d.*1915, of Grey Scar, Spittal	WILLIAM *m.* TALLENTIRE (gt grandfather) of North Side, Bowes	ANNE SAYER (grandmother)	Thomas *b.*1832, *d.*1909

James

saac 1856, 935, of mmah Hill	William *b.*1868, *d.*1934, of Low Birk Hatt	John Robert Norman Bayles (2nd cousin) *m.* Lizzie Teasdale of Mickleton

olet	Mary Anne	Maggie *d.*1919	Sarah *d.*1919	Isaac Thomas *d.*1919	Richard

INTRODUCTION

The message on my desk from a Yorkshire Television researcher was brief and very much to the point:

'Some friend of mine hiking the Pennine Way met a woman called Hannah Hauxwell living alone on an isolated farm in Baldersdale. No electricity, no water, good talker, could be worth a look!'

Alone, with neither water nor electricity? It was early summer in 1972 and I was putting together ideas for a series tentatively titled 'The Hard Life'. This lady's life sounded pretty hard.

Since the opening of Yorkshire Television in 1968 I had been working the Yorkshire Dales as often as possible. Urban life had no appeal for me so I began to make short films among the hill farmers and other Dales characters for inclusion in *Calendar*, the daily news and current affairs programme for the region we served. This thread developed into a regional series of twenty-to-thirty-minute programmes called *Country Calendar*, which had an immediate and very gratifying impact on the viewers. The local Press began to comment very favourably, and *Yorkshire Life* magazine even invited me to write about my films. Other independent television stations began to transmit them, so gradually they went network, coast to coast across the country.

Consequently, the head of the documentary department, John Fairley, and I sat down to try and analyse what it was about *Country Calendar* which had appealed to the public. What was the essence? John Fairley pinpointed it . . . it appeared in his judgement that it was to do with hardship and loneliness. Sequences featuring shepherds spilling sweat on the fells, Dalesfolk suffering extremes of weather as a matter of course, small people in a huge, beautiful but often hazardous landscape had excited the interest of viewers and television journalists alike. A phenomenally large postbag reinforced this view. So I was charged to seek out more Dalesfolk who lived a hard and lonely life. I briefed researchers in the department to let me know if they picked up any leads.

Thus, when I am asked (and it happens frequently) how I ever managed to find Hannah Hauxwell, a totally unknown figure at the top of an isolated and mainly abandoned Yorkshire dale, I can honestly say that I was, in a way, specifically looking for her, or people like her.

I very nearly didn't find her, as it turned out. That memo on my desk led me to the bottom of Baldersdale on one blustery July day. It looked a very empty place. Driving slowly along I came across a solitary figure examining the quality of his grass (it was nearly time to cut the hay) and solicited his aid.

'Hannah Hauxwell? Eh, lad! She lives at a place called Low Birk Hatt, but it's right near the top of the dale. Tha'll nivver find 'er!'

But I kept trying. I travelled some miles further along a road which wound sinuously along a truly attractive dale (and by then I was something of a connoisseur) augmented by the glistening waters of what I took to be a lake (it was actually Hury Reservoir, which wanders at length). Then I came across a sign which marked the Pennine Way, but it was pointing towards the high moors, where only Swaledale sheep can survive. Clearly that was the wrong way, so I began to follow the route in the opposite direction, abandoning the car when the unmown grass and rutted track began to scrape heavily against the exhaust system. By necessity, I had to climb over several dry-stone walls which were crumbling from a generation's neglect, dislodging the occasional half hundredweight on to my shins, and came to a ridge. The prospect it revealed was distinctly unpromising. I could see two farmsteads in the distance, and both appeared to be abandoned. The sky had darkened ominously, and the kind of keen breeze which presages rain sprang up.

I considered the situation carefully, and came close to abandoning the project and seeking prospects other than this Hannah Hauxwell from a fairly long list. But I plunged over yet another trembling dry-stone wall and chose, for no particular reason, to head for the farm on the left.

The nearer I approached, the less promising it became. There was no smoke issuing from the chimneys, the paths were overgrown, the slate roof of the barn was in a state of disrepair, and there was neither sight nor sound of life.

Quite suddenly a curious figure appeared from the rear of the farmhouse and began walking towards a pile of stones in the middle of the side pasture. A woman with hair as white as a pensioner's, wearing what appeared to be several layers of carefully laundered rags. It was a sight which stopped me short. I watched spellbound for a moment – she hadn't noticed me – then cleared my throat and said, 'Er . . . Miss Hauxwell?'

She reacted like a roe deer on hearing an approaching predator, appearing to levitate about two feet in the air. I thought for an instant that she was going to flee across the fields, taking the boundary walls in her stride. I was not aware at this time that her life was so solitary that she could go two weeks without seeing a soul.

Hastily, I explained who I was, and the nature of my visit. She relaxed immediately and smiled in that seraphic way which would later transfer to celluloid and stir the emotions of a large section of the English-speaking world. The greeting she extended was delightfully antiquated, almost Victorian, in its mannerisms. She talked animatedly, clearly eager for conversation, and showed me around her house as she innocently described an extraordinary lifestyle, totally devoid of the comforts and standards everyone else takes for granted. The farmhouse was lit by oil lamps, the water was drawn from a stream running forty yards from her front door. Further upstream, a cow up to its hocks in the same water . . .

A couple of mesmeric hours later, I bade her farewell, and began the long trek back to Leeds and the Yorkshire Television studios. This time I knew I had a film from the Yorkshire Dales which would go straight on to the network.

But nobody at that stage, however fevered the imagination, could have forecast the impact Hannah Bayles Tallentire Hauxwell would have on the public.

ONE

Baldersdale
– A Classic Yorkshire Dale

Baldersdale, one of the tributary valleys of Teesdale, has been home to the various branches of the Hauxwell family for several (maybe countless) generations. It is a Yorkshire dale in a classic sense with sweeping contours and a fierce beauty on the grand scale, although in recent years it has been placed in County Durham (not that locals pay any attention to such cultural vandalism). But Baldersdale does have one extra visual blessing rarely seen in the Dales – water. Hury Reservoir was built a century or so ago and it stretches sinuously up a major portion of the valley. The eastern fells are reflected along its surface by day and the moon by night. The only other substantial piece of water in the western dales is Lake Semer Water, near Bainbridge, in Upper Wensleydale.

Baldersdale possesses another significant factor – it is a closed place. You can enter from the main road running along Teesdale but there is no way through at the top of the dale, unless you travel on horseback, or on foot, if you possess the stamina and know how to use a compass. No one just passes through Baldersdale, and this clearly played a major part in preserving its isolation in the days when it was a full and vibrant community, as, indeed, it certainly was. Today the place echoes with emptiness, its brown stone dwellings and farmhouses mainly abandoned, some neglected and crumbling, others no longer in existence. There are no children to educate so the schoolhouse is now a youth centre, the chapel no longer has its worshippers, the pub is now a farm.

But Hannah can vividly recall Baldersdale in its finest days, as a place where the full theatre of life was played out. She can even recall the minutiae which put flesh on the bones of memory – speech mannerisms, individual eccentricities and habits, clothing, names (even nicknames), hairstyles . . . everything. She builds up a full and fascinating portrait of a community with an acute sense of history which gives her descriptions a unique dimension.

As Hannah moves fluently along her journey into the past, what emerges most strongly to the listener is a sense of privilege – that here is a survivor of a lost way of life which was so innocent and simple, so materially deprived, yet spiritually rich, that it might have been part of another civilization altogether, surviving from an earlier century, perhaps. Such was their isolation that their way of life hardly reflected at all the kind to be found just a dozen miles away. Baldersdale was largely unaffected by contact with outside influences – to travel further than Barnard Castle, a prim and pretty little market town which could scarcely claim to be cosmopolitan, was virtually unheard of, and such visitors as there were never stayed long enough to impart revolutionary new ways and ideas. The horse and not the internal-combustion engine provided the principal method of transport, and day-to-day living was based on unremitting toil and self-sacrifice. The land they tilled and the animals they raised absorbed most of their working hours. It was a constant battle, fuelled by the basic survival instinct which kept men moving ahead over thousands of years towards what we are pleased to call modern civilization today. In Baldersdale that process gathered no speed at all and, indeed, never even crossed the finishing line.

The entire community was also welded together by two other elements. The knowledge that the only help you could expect in times of trouble or need would have to be sought from a near neighbour; and, even more fundamental, the bond of blood. Dalesfolk around the first half of the century tended to marry within their close community, so nearly everyone was related to nearly everyone else. Hannah's parents were half-cousins and there were many convoluted relationships. For instance, in Chapter Five of this book Hannah records that her piano teacher's father and her, that is Hannah's, grandmother were cousins! How on earth that evolved is probably a relativity equation comparable with Einstein's.

A century ago, Baldersdale had a population numbering several hundred and supported a blacksmith, two pubs and even a small flour mill. It had declined substantially by the late thirties but was still a thriving place compared with the Baldersdale of today.

Oh yes, Baldersdale was a busy place in my childhood, full of people. There was always someone in the next field to say 'Hello' to, and the school, which had two teachers, usually had more than thirty children in attendance. There must have been more than twenty farms, plus the school, the chapel and the Strathmore Arms. They used to hold Hury Show in a field alongside the pub, and there was a wooden hut called the Show Room to be used on the big day, where dances were also held on a regular basis.

Low Birk Hatt Farm has always been home for my family. No one else has ever lived here. Although I was born at Sleetburn further up the dale, I came here when I was three years old, so I do not recall any other place as home. We used to rent it from the Kipling

family before Daddy bought it, but even my great-grandfather William Bayles farmed at Low Birk Hatt.*
It was a mixed farm, with cattle, sheep and geese. I remember my uncle Tommy Hauxwell, who came to live with us to manage the farm after Father died, telling me about the time Great-Grandad bought a big flock of geese over in Stainmore, which is more than six miles away over the moors. And he drove them home all the way, presumably with the help of his dogs. Uncle said he will never forget as a little boy the sight of all these geese coming over the hill beyond our top pasture.

He must have been quite an enterprising business-man, my great-grandad, because he ran the butter cart in Baldersdale. It was red in colour and had much bigger wheels than the ordinary farm cart. A mare called Smiler used to pull it, and he would collect all the butter and eggs in the dale to take to Barnard Castle. He would call on some farms and others would bring what they had to sell down to Low Birk Hatt. I've heard that this farm was a very busy place on Tuesday nights and Wednesday mornings and the kitchen would be piled high with eggs and butter. Then Great-Grandad would drive the lot down to

* The Kiplings probably built and certainly owned Low Birk Hatt, but never lived there, according to Hannah.

Barnard Castle to get the best price he could in the marketplace.

People would turn up again in large numbers on Wednesday nights to be paid for their produce. Naturally Great-Grandad would take a share, a sort of commission for his trouble, if you like. And he would bring back goods from the market, such as meal, and sell or exchange that for what the Dalesfolk had brought. The old system of barter, I suppose.

Great-Grandfather was running a farm at the same time, so he must have been a very busy man. And life was quite a struggle for everyone, it seems. I'm going back now to before the First World War, sometime in the early years of this century. But I do know that when times were bad, the people in the dale had to use the wool off the backs of the sheep themselves instead of sending it away to the wool merchants of Bradford after shearing. They would make more money that way.

We had a spinning wheel at Low Birk Hatt – it may be still around the place somewhere – and the whole family would spin the raw wool and then knit it into stockings, gloves, jumpers and skirts. I do believe that in years gone by they paid the annual rent for Low Birk Hatt by spinning and knitting.

Eventually the Kiplings put Low Birk Hatt up for sale and there is a sad and curious story associated with this. It concerns my great-aunt Jane Bayles, who was my father's mother's sister and lived at Hury at the bottom of the dale. She was both a clever woman and a fool at one and the same time. Her sister, my great-aunt Margaret Bayles, married a Dalesman called George Brown, and lived at Blackton Farm. They hired a man with red hair called John Bell to catch the moles which were plaguing their land. From what I can gather he was as mad as a hatter, and really no good at all. He was what we called 'a hook', which means a slippery fish.

Anyway, Great-Aunt Jane shared everyone's low opinion of John Bell for a time, even going as far as to declare that he wasn't right in his head. And then, would you believe it, she went and married him. I gather from the little bits of information which came my way that the match was a disaster. I do know that he outlived Great-Aunt Jane and he made a lot of trouble by claiming items of property to which he had no right. He brought nothing at all into the marriage, and the family wanted nothing to do with him. I heard that Uncle Tommy was in Barnard Castle one day when someone asked him, 'Are ye owt 'a kin to yon John Bell?' Uncle denied it and when challenged said, 'Aye, he might have wed my aunt but that doesn't mek 'm owt 'a kin to me.' He was a real pest, and thank goodness he and Great-Aunt Jane had no children.

But Great-Aunt Jane did a very strange thing. My father and mother were living at Sleetburn, where I was born, with my grandparents and a great-uncle, when Low Birk Hatt came up for auction. Daddy wanted that farm very badly but they didn't have much money between them, so he had to go to the bank and ask for a loan. And then – what a lunatic thing to do – Great-Aunt Jane began to bid against my father at the auction for Low Birk Hatt. Uncle Tommy always said that there was insanity in the family, so that incident proves it, if nothing else.

Goodness only knows why she did it, but it put the price up, of course. It was knocked down to Father for £1,600, which in those days – it was the 1920s – was a very high price. I do know that he became very depressed when the times were bad and he had the mortgage payments to meet. It was a great struggle for him and we all suffered because of it.

Oddly enough my father allowed Great-Aunt Jane and John Bell to live at Low Birk Hatt after he had bought it. I cannot imagine why. But I do know *that* great-aunt was not exactly popular after the incident of the farm sale, and eventually John Bell left her so her brother, Great-Uncle William, came to work the farm.

It was always considered necessary for a man to shoulder the main burden of work at a farm the size of ours, and I suppose the main reason why the place is a bit run down these days is because there was no man left to take over when Uncle died. I had to do it all by myself.

TWO

Portrait of an Enclosed Community

As these family dramas were played out around Low Birk Hatt Farm and the Hauxwell family battled against the twin effects of an overpriced, heavily mortgaged farm, and an agricultural depression which presaged the deep national depression of the thirties, the other people in Baldersdale coped with their lives. Hannah recalls the people, the personalities and the events in fine detail.

Balder Head was the highest farm in the dale, as the name suggests, and a family called Green lived there. Husband and wife and three boys, and later on they had a little girl. It was a small farm and I think Mr Green had to work away from home sometimes to bring a bit more money in. I do believe it was forestry work that he did.

The boys were younger than me but I remember them coming to school – and what a job that was for them. They had to walk, and a real hike it was – getting on for three miles, I think. Eventually their father came to some arrangement with the Education Authority and he was able to afford a small car to drive them to school.

I only went once to visit the Greens and then I was collecting money for the Missionary Fund to which most people contributed a copper or two, with young Mrs Thwaites from the neighbouring farm to us, High Birk Hatt. Balder Head farmhouse was so close to the reservoir that the water lapped up to the garden wall. The place is no longer there now, but it wasn't one of the several that fell down after being abandoned. It was taken away stone by stone and rebuilt in part at the Beamish Museum in the Newcastle area, which specializes in preserving country ways. So Balder Head must have had some architectural significance or other, although I doubt if anyone in the dale realized it.

The next farm down was West Carnigill where Mr and Mrs Addison, Jack and Madge, lived. Mrs Addison was a bonny woman with a mass of dark hair which she wore in a coil. Sadly she wasn't blessed with good health – in fact, neither was Mr Addison – and they had no children. But they stayed the longest in Baldersdale, apart from me, of course, and eventually retired down to Hunderthwaite, down near the main road.

Near to them was East Carnigill and the Bellerbys. They had three children, Doris who was a bit older

than me, Jim a bit younger, and a little chap called
Ernest. Doris and Jim went to school at the same time
as me.

Then there was Foul Syke, where a man called
Lance Sowerby lived. I have a feeling that he had been
married but I do not know what happened. I used to
see him at Chapel Anniversary, and my uncle would
say that he was a romancer, meaning that in the nicer
way. He could spin a yarn, and you had to take what
he said with a pinch of salt.

After that came Sleetburn, where I was born on
1 August 1926, which was owned by a William Hutchinson when we lived there. We were followed by Mr
and Mrs Atkinson, their son Douglas, and Mrs Atkinson's two sisters, the Misses Elizabeth and Annabella
Hind. Now this was a family I was very close to
eventually when they became quite near neighbours in
later years by moving to Clove Lodge, just up the
pasture from Low Birk Hatt. I used to go and stay
there at Christmastime, after Father died, and there
was always a nice present on the juniper tree for me
and lots of good things to eat. We had stopped
celebrating Christmas in the proper manner after
Father died. I suppose we really couldn't afford to.

They had been followed to Sleetburn by the Wil-
kinson family, who had moved from West Thorngarth
Hill down the dale at Hury because they needed a

bigger farm, I seem to remember. They had a son and a daughter, Sidney and Agnes.

Well, now we come to West Birk Hatt and the Fawcett family, and really wonderful people they were. Such a lot of them too, with eight children, as well as a resident relative. Let me see, there would be Mary and Ellen, two older daughters who were soon to move away, and then Neddy, Sidney, George, Dick, Sepp, and eventually Geoffrey. Sepp was really Septimus, the seventh, and I called one of my calves the same name.

Mr Sam Fawcett was a truly remarkable man, and if he were alive today would be a television and radio personality, I am certain. Indeed he did broadcast on the BBC before the war with a man called Harry Hopeful who ran a very popular show, rather on the same lines as Wilfrid Pickles and his *Have a Go* programme. Sam could sing and play the concertina and violin, and he must have been good for the BBC to come all the way to Baldersdale to find him. I wonder how that happened.

I know he would regularly come down to Low Birk Hatt – and, indeed, Sleetburn when we were there – with his violin, and Mother used to accompany him on our organ. They spent hours together, particularly when one or the other had acquired a new piece of music. I recall one man in the dale saying that he passed Sleetburn going up the fell to shepherd at

10 a.m. one day and heard Sam and Mother playing. He came back at 3 p.m. and they were still going.

Wherever the Fawcetts were you would hear music. It was lovely on the hot summer nights listening to the sound of the various instruments being played at West Birk Hatt, drifting half a mile across the valley. Sam had a bachelor brother called Tom, known as Tuck, who had silver hair and beard. He was a very good sheep man and had been known to tap dance, but only on very rare and special occasions.

Sam was also a keen and talented naturalist. What he didn't know about birds, foxes, moles and all the other creatures of the fields wasn't worth knowing. Of course, he had been brought up to it because his father, Edmund Fawcett, was a gamekeeper. That was before my time, of course, but he obviously passed on some of his skills because during, or just after, very wet weather, Sam would go off somewhere and catch lovely brown trout, which he often gave to people who were ill; and sometimes when he had a sheep to kill, he would send down the head which would make a really tasty and nourishing broth. His garden was a credit to him, too, and he grew flowers and potatoes. He would also give those away, and I remember when my poor father died he brought down one, if not two, lovely lilies which Mother put in a slender silver vase. He was such a loyal, staunch and tender-hearted friend of my family, and such an outgoing man. He laughed a lot and his laugh would boom down the dale. He used to come over to us a lot at weekends, along with another character called Bob Brown, who lived at Blackton and who was a bachelor brother of my great-aunt's husband. He was a very decent man but had not been blessed with all the faculties one would normally expect.

Anyway, they would land down at our place most weekends, because we used to take the *Darlington and Stockton Times*, and they would all be smoking their pipes and talking, asking, 'What hast thou fresh, now?' and catching up on the comings and goings of Baldersdale. They were grand folk, and it's because of them that I am not one of the antismoking lobby, although I have never associated personally with nicotine. It's just that I have such happy pictures in my mind of those times that pipes will always have nice associations for me.

Another thing we had which would attract the locals to call was a weather glass – a barometer, most people would call it, I suppose, and I still have it on my wall. They would visit to see what it was doing at particular times, like haymaking.

Mrs Fawcett, Sam's wife, was another grand person. She and Mother were the best of friends, and she knew that I was daft over dollies and wanted one so badly.

Anyhow, she set to and found the time to make one for me, even though she had such a large family to care for. The body was made from the strong cotton bags that the flour came in, she worked some black fur for its hair, and stuffed it with straw or some old hay. Then with her needle she worked eyebrows, eyes and mouth, and made a dress out of an old dress that belonged to one of her girls. I can picture it now, a fine velvet cord and such bonny colours. Septimus brought it down for me one Christmastime when I was just a girl – before the last war, anyhow. Septimus was younger than me and not very big and he could scarcely carry this big lovely dolly. I cherished that dolly, kept on altering the face with new stitching from time to time, and I still have it in a drawer somewhere.

I really do not know where Mrs Fawcett found the energy to do what she did. I seem to recall that she baked a stone of flour a week making bread and teacakes to keep all those mouths fed. I heard that she lost one baby as well, and I do know that she suffered badly with her legs, varicose veins, I believe. Sad thing was she had been a noted dancer in her day. It was quite usual to see her standing there baking, one knee on a cushion placed on a stool, to ease the pain.

I have very affectionate memories of Sidney, one of the elder Fawcett boys. Uncle got a white dog from him once, a very unusual colour for a farm dog. It was exchanged later for a black Old English sheepdog owned by some relatives of ours at Piercebridge. Sidney pretended to be upset about this – at least I think he was pretending – because he said to Uncle, 'A 's not friends wi' thee now – thee's parted wi' my white dog.'

Sidney was a tall young man like his brother George. When war came in 1939, Sidney went into the Coldstream Guards and George into the Grenadier Guards. They would come back on leave and wear their scarlet tunics in the dale. I can see them in my mind's eye even now. They were grand boys and so courageous . . . maybe too much so as it turned out.

You see, I'm sad to say that Sidney never came back. He was taken prisoner in Italy and tried to escape, I understand. The Fawcett family were very brave about it when the telegram came from the War Office. Oh dear, that was a black day in Baldersdale. Believe me, we all had a warm place in our hearts for Sidney.

George was taken prisoner, too, when he was fighting in France, and I remember reading in a newspaper how he had escaped as well. He had been at large in occupied France and had quite a tough time of it, but at least he survived and came back to Baldersdale.

Mind, the Fawcett family's association with the dale had a sad ending, because Mr Fawcett died, and then their farm, West Birk Hatt, disappeared when they built the extension to the reservoir at Balder Head. What's left of it is many yards under water now.

The closest people to us in terms of distance were the Thwaites, just at the top of our main pasture, in High Birk Hatt. Here again, the lady of the house was so kind and resourceful. The husband was called Jack, and everyone called him by his first name, but for some reason one always called his wife Mrs Thwaites, although we all knew her Christian name was Margaret. It was just one of those things that you cannot explain.

They had two daughters, Violet and Madge, and two sons, Luther and John. Both girls were keen cyclists and since they lived near the road they could get out and about. They both married, with Madge going to live in Cotherstone, just about the nearest village to us, and Violet staying near the bottom of the dale. Luther did leave the community for good, going off to work in Darlington, where he married and settled down.

When the elders at our place began to fall ill, Mrs Thwaites was the best neighbour we could have. She was such a hard worker and a wonderful cook. She would send over beef tea and other delicacies to try and cheer them up. They were good to me, too, and I recall young John Thwaites being sent down to our farm one Christmas with such a big rosy red apple that I can close my eyes and still see it now. And when I went to play occasionally near to their house, Mrs Thwaites would bring out large sweet biscuits for me. She was really good at baking.

We had four elderly people to look after at Low Birk Hatt, my father's parents and two uncles. That meant that there were seven mouths to feed, and then Daddy began to ail.

When the elder members of the family began to die, Mrs Thwaites did most, if not all, of the baking and catering for the funerals. The undertaker was Mr Alan Anderson from the firm of Raines, joiners of Mickleton, who would carry out his duties with great delicacy, sympathy and understanding.

We used to get our hay rakes from the same firm, and they were so beautifully made – light and easy to work with. I still have one or two but they are near the end of their useful life.

There was another family in the dale which, like us, lost their father and mainstay at an early age. They were the Sayers over at West New Houses, a big place with a sheep moor which belonged to the Strathmores, the Queen Mother's family.

It was a big undertaking, this farm, with hired hands on a permanent basis, so they were pretty well off by the standards of Baldersdale. Mr and Mrs Sayers had five children, but only one son, John. Then Mr Sayers died prematurely when John was only about fifteen, so he was still just a boy when he had to become a man overnight, so to speak, and try and take on the running of this large and rather complicated farm. The entire future of the family and the farm fell on his shoulders, and what a wonderful job he made of it. He was always so quick-witted and courageous, was John, that I always thought he would have made a good secret agent – a James Bond kind of figure. He had such energy and drive, and liked to play hard as well as work hard, and had a few scrapes with his motorbike. The girls were called Lizzie, Winnie, Ada and Edith, and I think all of them got married. John married later on, too.

Over at Hill Gill Farm there was another lady who had musical talent – Mrs Annie Bainbridge. This was a rather isolated place, tucked behind a hill, and she used to run a little shop, probably for the company as much as anything. I know she became somewhat lonely because her husband, although he was a very hard worker, would go off on a spree for some days at a time. They weren't badly off because I do believe they ran a car and she would wear a lovely fox fur when she was out and about in the dale. She would wear it for Chapel Anniversary, I would think, because that was a very special occasion in Baldersdale. I can still bring it to mind, with lines of people coming off the hillsides and on to the road. They would bring their relations, too, and there would always be visiting preachers and singers who used to stay in the dale – we would always find room for our special visitors.

The chapel was only a single-storey affair and for anniversaries and other big events they used to make extra seats by placing bars of wood between one seat and the next. I used to enjoy the singing a lot but sometimes the preachers used to go on quite a bit. Just when you thought they were about to finish they would burst off again. It was too much for a little girl and I think it rather put me off chapel. And then we would get the evangelists staying for a fortnight at a time, holding services every night asking people to come forward and rededicate themselves. I have to say I didn't really care much for that kind of approach.

Then in wintertime we had a Guild meeting every Tuesday night with various people taking turns to organize it. I would recite some of the lines Grandad had taught me and sometimes sing songs like 'Won't You Buy My Pretty Flowers?'. Once after I had recited at the Guild I was given a pair of woollen gloves, speckled coloured, and with cuffs, which was quite an unexpected treat.

The chapel is closed nowadays, and the school is a youth centre. At one time there would be more than thirty children and two teachers. The senior was Mrs Archer, who lived in the schoolhouse with her husband

and daughter, Bessie, who joined the ATS in the war. She was assisted by Miss Walker, whom I liked very much, and I was so sad when she left to get married.

Now Mrs Archer was a very good woman in her way but I'm afraid that I was never one of her favourites because I was so slow to catch on, particularly in mathematics. I cannot say that my school days were particularly happy ones and I was not sorry to leave when I got to the official leaving age, which was fourteen in those days.

That was not long after the Second World War broke out. But I was still at school when the evacuees arrived mostly from Newcastle and Sunderland, so they would be safe from German air raids. They brought one or two of their own teachers with them, and farms which had the room to spare took them in as boarders.

The schoolchildren were split into seven standards or classes but we only had one room and one blackboard. It must have been difficult for the teachers to organize things even before the arrival of the evacuees, who had problems of their own, of course, adjusting to a major change in lifestyle. We would be split into different groups, with perhaps ten sitting round the blackboard for one lesson and the others in another part of the room working at something else. There were two fireplaces, one at each end of the classroom, two large cupboards and the teacher's desk was on the north wall.

The school day always began with prayers at nine o'clock, followed by a scripture lesson, and there was invariably arithmetic in some form or another until dinnertime. The rest of the time was devoted to history or geography, but always there would be two afternoons given over to handicrafts, particularly knitting and sewing. Even the boys had to knit. We also had looms and were taught weaving, basketwork and raffia. The day finished at 3.30 p.m.

We took our own sandwiches for lunch and a teacher would boil a kettle so we could make tea or cocoa for ourselves. There was no need for free milk like other schoolchildren received, because most of us came from farms with cows, so we brought our own.

There weren't many facilities for games, but the boys used to kick a football about the yard, and the girls played rounders. In later years some swings were put up for the school, but that was after my time.

Of course, I enjoyed the company at school because my childhood was a bit lonely. There were no brothers and sisters for me to play with, and the only one I could really call a playmate was Derek Brown, who lived just ten minutes away from Low Birk Hatt at Blackton Farm. Derek's mother was my great-aunt's daughter, which I think made him a half-cousin to me.

He used to call for me to go to school, and that could be an eventful journey because the way led through the Sayers' farm at West New Houses, and they kept a flock of geese and a bull.

They were careful to keep the bull in the same field much of the time but sometimes they would have to move him and occasionally he would get out, so one always had to be wary. But I was also terrified of the geese because of a childhood experience – I was chased by a flock and the memory always stayed with me. They can really hurt you, particularly the ganders because they have such strong wings. So it was rather a question of running the gauntlet when passing over the Sayers' land. Trouble was, I could never run very quickly, and I cannot imagine what I would have done if I had been chased by the bull. Now, they are really dangerous and I understand that even today they are responsible for a number of deaths and serious accidents each year among farm workers. As far as I can recall there were no unfortunate incidents involving animals in Baldersdale. Bad weather took more of a toll in our community and Derek Brown's family suffered a tragedy during one bad winter. Their only son at the time, a cousin of my father's called William Bayles Brown, went out on Cotherstone Moor in a snowstorm to gather up some sheep, and never came back. A search party found him the next day, dead from exposure. They could tell from his footprints in the snow that he had been trying to find a ford, which is what we call a stone shelter built for gathering sheep. His body was found very close to it, but he had obviously been blinded by the blizzard. He might have survived if only he could have found it. The poor man left a widow and a young daughter.

A newspaper account of this incident makes fascinating reading, written as it is in the florid, expansive style of the day to extract every ounce of drama. It was a triple headline: 'TRAGIC DEATH ON A TEESDALE MOOR . . . SHEPHERD VANQUISHED IN A RAGING STORM . . . FATEFUL VIGIL OF A SHEEPDOG'. It goes on:

'The story of the death of William Bayles Brown, only son of George and Margaret Brown of Blackton, Baldersdale, is a weird narrative of the melancholy end of a courageous shepherd on a high moor in Teesdale . . . at eleven o'clock last Thursday morning the deceased left home in an endeavour to bring the high moor sheep to shelter . . . went off, whistling aloud, in the direction of the ill-fated higher common. He was soon fully a mile on the moor, a terrible doom, forsooth, awaiting him. There had been a phenomenally heavy snowstorm in Baldersdale, and especially on the loftier peaks. There were found footprint evidences that young Brown had crossed and recrossed Hunder Beck, that he had been at the top of the high moor, and he was traced half way back, with probably thirty-six sheep which were recovered on Sunday. It was in the gloaming on Thursday that the brave young fellow's father became alarmed by reason of his son not returning, and the distressed parent went to see a neighbour. As a matter of fact, he called upon Mr Fawcett and unburthened [sic] his apprehensions . . . Deceased's father, with Thomas Hawkswell [sic] set out as a search party, and eventually traced the "footings" of the missing man . . . to the old Groove house, and found the lifeless body of young Brown lying just outside the dilapidated building, with his faithful dog watching over the remains of its departed master . . . the deceased had been married about nine months but he, however, resided with his father at Blackton, while his wife lived with her mother at Bowes, pending their securing a farm and home to themselves, a consummation well within sight at the time of this untoward happening – this mysterious interposition, which surely intimates eternity to man . . .'

The Bayles were quite plentiful in the dale for many years – my great-great-grandfather was a John Bayles –

but they have all gone now, except me. I am the only one left in Baldersdale with Bayles blood in my veins.

The main branch of the Bayles family farmed at New Houses. The head of the family when I first remember them was William Henry Bayles, who was Grandmother's cousin and the father of a lady who taught me a little bit of music. She was their only daughter. Then there was William Henry's wife Mary, and his niece, Mary Hannah, who unfortunately lost both parents when she was young and came to make her home with them. The farm had originally been two or three houses and there was a little cottage at the back where a lady we used to call Aunt Polly lived. She was William Henry's sister, and it was such a nice place. We would visit her on occasions and I remember she had a rather splendid grandfather clock. The Bayles and the Tallentires were related by marriage. Great-Great-Grandfather Tallentire had a daughter called Hannah who became a Bayles when she married and who was my father's grandmother. Her brother was William Tallentire and he became my mother's grandfather, which meant that my mother and father were akin. It probably made them half-cousins. Then there was a great-great-grandmother Elizabeth Tallentire, who was Grandmother Bayles's grandmother, who lived with her husband at a farm over at Holwick, which is a little way out of Baldersdale, on the way to Middleton in Teesdale. Now Great-Great-Grand-mother Elizabeth must have been a very capable woman because circumstances demanded that her husband went out to work as a miner, so she was left to manage the farm. And she had six children yet still found time to appreciate music, a very strong trait of the Tallentires.

Sad to say that there was a disaster in her family too, which was once again caused by the weather. A group of people had just finished haytiming at a farm called Pikestone, in Holwick, and began to cross the swing bridge across the Tees. Apparently there must have been very heavy rain higher up the dale because there had been some flooding and the river was running very fast. The story goes that it was a very merry party – maybe they were celebrating being able to get in the hay after a bad spell – and they stepped on the bridge to enjoy some music, a very Tallentire thing to do. Anyhow, the bridge collapsed and a number were drowned, including, I believe, one of Great-Great-Grandmother's sons, Thomas Tallentire.

Haymaking, now that was an important event in the life of the dale – still is for me – because that's when you harvest the fodder for the animals when winter comes and there is no grazing to be had. Lambing time is even more important because lambs are a cash crop and nobody ever had an abundance of that.

I can still hear in my imagination the sounds of lambing in springtime, particularly from Blind Beck, just over to the north-east from us where the Lowsons farmed. John and Elsie they were called, and they had two sons, Stanley and Gilbert. Grandfather Lowson lived with them – he was called Matthew, nicknamed Mather – and he was a character who could tell a good story.

The Lowsons were reckoned to be very good farmers and they were very up to date. There was such a racket from their place at night during lambing time – and that's a twenty-four-hour job with no time to sleep. They had the modern aluminium racks on wheels for foddering the sheep instead of the traditional, very much more silent version made from wood. Well, the lids of these racks rattled like mad as they put the hay in to feed the sheep after they had given birth. So with that and all the shouting at each other and the dogs, lambing time was extremely noisy.

Mind, the Lowsons stuck to the old ways in other respects. During wintertime John Lowson was rarely seen without his hessian sacks. Now, the old-fashioned, strong hessian is wonderful for keeping you warm and dry and John always sported three sacks – one round his waist, another over his shoulders, and the third with the corner pushed in for a hood over his head.

The Lowsons farmed Blind Beck for a number of

generations. John's grandmother, Betty Hind, lived there and she was quite famous in the dale as someone you did not trifle with. Not a battleaxe exactly, but I hear she used to stomp around the place in clogs and speak her mind without fear or hesitation.

At the end of the reservoir dam there used to be a place called Blackton House which was rather crowded. It was where Fred Sowerby and his wife lived, and they had seven children, Teresa, Eric, Ruth, Gertie, Norman, Mabel and Pat. Mr Sowerby worked for the Water Board and unfortunately was permanently affected by an injury sustained in the First World War. There was some shrapnel in one of his legs which they had never been able to get out. Poor man, he dropped down dead just at the beginning of the terrible winter of 1947.

Sadly their house doesn't exist any more. It was just left abandoned like so many of the others and fell into a state of disrepair. The authorities decided it was dangerous so it had to be knocked down.

Another place across the dale from us was East New Houses, where a maiden lady lived when I was a child. She was Miss Sarah Anne Walker, an only child left to cope on her own when both her mother and father died. But the family had been comfortably off, and she was able to hire hands to run the farm. Anyhow, a man called Jack Foster, who came from round Middleton way, was employed as her farm manager, and ended up marrying Miss Walker. I remember the wedding and I do believe that Mr Foster was a bit younger than she, but he was a very sincere and deeply caring person. I do know that they were both very kind to their hired help and treated one or two more like sons than employees. They would let them stay on until they married and got farms of their own, because, perhaps, their own home circumstances would not be very good. Miss Walker was a mature lady when she married, if my memory serves me correctly, and they never had children of their own.

There were some other Walkers at Brier Dykes who were related to Miss Sarah Anne. Thomas and Agnes Walker, they were called, and they had a son called Tommy, who was a good deal older than me, and two daughters who had married and left the dale before my memory of Baldersdale begins. They were God-fearing folk and attended Sunday services regularly, he a very quiet man, and she a rather stout and well-built lady. Tommy was married before the war and raised a family.

Over at the west end of Hury there was a house which had been a pub called the Hare and Hounds, occupied by a family who were rather special to me. There was a widow-lady called Mrs Raw and her son Bernard, who shared their home with an elderly gentleman, Mr William Wilkins. We used to call him Daddy Wilkins because he was the father of a large family, but they had all grown up, got married and spread about, so he was left on his own – probably not able to cook for himself, which is why he went to live at Mrs Raw's place. She was such a nice, kind lady and I recall her taking care of me on one of the Sunday School trips when Mother was unable to go. And I had an affection for Bernard who went to school with me. Although he was three or four years older, he was always thoughtful and friendly towards me, never unkind, when, perhaps, some of the other pupils were not as pleasant. You see, I would be teased a lot at school because I may not have been as quick as the others, but Bernard never joined in. He had a favourite song he used to sing in the old days – 'It's a Sin to Tell a Lie' – and I shall always associate it with him.

Close to the Raws' was another house called Dovers where an elderly couple called Bell lived, and just over the wall from there was Nelson House where Grandfather and Grandmother Hauxwell lived before they moved to Sleetburn. The next family to occupy Nelson House was the Linds, who were friends of my family. They had a son William, and a daughter Margaret, and a niece of Mrs Lind called Marjorie also lived with them. The father, David, had two nice Dales horses called Bonnie and Bess, both good, thickset animals.

Mr Lind used to ride Bess and, on occasion, would lend us Bonnie. The Linds are resident at Nelson House even to this day. I'm afraid that William died, but his wife and son Keith are still there with Keith's wife, Maureen, and their daughter, Catherine.

Further along the north side of Baldersdale there's Thorngarth Hill where the Wilkinsons lived before they moved to Sleetburn. They were followed by the Kiplings when they retired from Clove Lodge, which had been in the family for generations. The Kiplings owned both places – and Low Birk Hatt in the early days, of course -- so they were well off by local stand-ards. Over the back was Howgill Grange, inhabited by another branch of the same Walker family mentioned previously. The father was John Henry Walker and there were two daughters, Ada and Florence. Ada was a particularly striking young lady, with a pale com-plexion contrasted by very dark hair.

Further up the same road there were even more Walkers, all related, living at Botany Farm – William and Annie with one daughter, Marjorie, who was a little bit older than me. We went to school together, went to the same dances and then she married a soldier during the war. He came from Cambridge, and I haven't heard of her for a number of years.

Then there was East Thorngarth Hill, and the Simpsons. They had just the one son, Cecil, but four daughters, Ella, Connie, Rance and Muriel. They were keen Chapel folk and used to bring masses of flowers to Sunday School Anniversary. I am sorry to say that some of them are dead now, and others have left the dale to live in Barnard Castle with their own families.

Of course, most people have left now – either died or moved away.

I'm afraid that's the story of Baldersdale today . . . the place they abandoned . . . the dale they left to die. No chapel, no school, no recreation room, no pub, no social life of any kind, really. The place was so full once, alive with activity and children. Baldersdale is an empty place now and all that remains for me are memories, sweet memories.

THREE

'Too Long a Winter'

They called the film they made about me *Too Long a Winter*, and I have to declare immediately that I do not care for winter at all, for neither mind nor body agrees with it. You could say that most winters in Baldersdale are too long, and every time we have a really bad one it takes something away from me in a physical sense. Saps one's strength, you could say. But if you are a farmer like me you cannot avoid winter, whatever your age or physical condition. The animals need foddering, so out you have to go, whether or not there's a storm brewing.

Of course, when one was a child many years ago winter could be an advantage, and if the storm was bad enough they had to close the school, which was wonderful. And I recall when I was much younger, when women didn't wear trousers at all, the novelty of putting on Uncle's knee breeches, jacket and coat, to go out to the fields.

Nowadays I consider that winter comes too early in Baldersdale and stays too long. The last really bad one was in 1978 when the electricity was off for four days. I had not had the benefit of that lovely electricity for long, but how I did miss it when it absented itself. Everything in the house froze solid – the water in the kettle, even my false teeth in a cup beside my bed. And my coat, my big army coat, which is forty years old now but still a good friend, and as strong as ever, became a remarkable sight. It became very wet as I carried water to the beasts because there were some very rough days and then it flared out and froze. I looked just like a crinoline lady.

Having no power was the greatest problem. The chimney is blocked so I couldn't light a fire to heat anything up and I went without a hot drink for those four days. I did get a little warm milk from Rosa (but I am not at all keen on milk) and the warmest place at Low Birk Hatt, in fact, was the cow byre. I think it will be the hay that increases the temperature.

I would go straight to bed after finishing my work with all my clothes on, including Uncle's old tweed coat and socks. It was not an experience I would wish to endure very often.

I remember well the moment when the electricity came back on. At the time I was mucking out the byre stalls, and piling the manure on top of my big heap when I saw the lights go on in the house. I have had the pleasure of seeing some welcome sights in my time, but that comes very near the top of the list.

Mind, the worst winter of all was 1947. It never seemed to end. And the entire thing was preceded by a death at one of the near farms, just before the first of the storms came.

The frost was so hard that everything went steel grey – the ground, the water and the sky. The blizzards just went on and on, day after day, blowing the snow about. We had to dig out every day, and if you didn't hurry getting water and bringing the cattle out to drink, the path you had just made would be filled in again. Eventually the snow was so deep that it filled in all the fields with only the top few inches of the wall sticking out. Some of those walls were six feet in height. And the snow was so hard with the frost that you could walk over it with safety. That was just about the only redeeming feature of that winter because it formed a kind of bridge which made walking up to the road a lot easier. We had coal to carry from the top pasture by the road where the coalman used to leave it, and I don't think it would have been possible but for that snow bridge.

Of course, I was a lot younger and more able to cope in 1947, and I wasn't alone – Father had died by then but there was Mother and Uncle. I had to help Uncle fetch the coal for us and some corn oats for Prince the colt, and a mare which was in foal. We used a sledge with Prince pulling it along. And it was going downhill over the hard packed snow which was the worst bit, with me acting as a brake, hauling on a rope to keep the sledge from running forward into the horse's heels. The sheep had the worst time, and not many survived 1947, although provisions for people and animals alike were dropped in by helicopter, and the Army forced a way through on the south side of the dale.

The hardships produced a wonderful spirit in the community. Everybody would help everybody else. It became known that we were perilously short of hay because the haytiming on our pastures had been very poor that summer and it was impossible to bring enough in on the horse-drawn sledge on the few occasions we were able to get out. But neighbours sent down what they had to spare. And the people who were farming Blind Beck at the time killed a pig and sent down a lovely pork pie to us. There were several similar examples of true neighbourliness.

Then I was able to help when young Mrs Thwaites at High Birk Hatt, our nearest neighbours, suffered terribly from toothache and needed to go to the nearest dentist, who was in Barnard Castle. I offered to go with her for company and safety really, since it was dangerous to go out alone in conditions like that. Anyway, I knew what she was going through since I had been obliged to have all my top teeth out just before the storms started because they ached so much. Indeed, it was March that year before I managed to obtain a false set, which meant I had to go through the entire winter without a tooth in the top of my mouth.

Mrs Thwaites and I followed the path made in the snow by the animals and managed to get out of the dale all right. But we made rather a mistake on the way back, and we were picked up by an Army lorry and taken to West Friar House on the south side and given hot tea and something to eat. We did land home eventually but I think Mrs Thwaites's folks were understandably worried, wondering where we had got to.

There were no serious incidents in the 1947 winter, such as people losing their way and dying of cold, although a Mr Sowerby on the other side of the dale died suddenly whilst helping a neighbour. I believe he had a heart attack. Funnily enough, we had just as much peril when the thaw came, because it was so rapid that it caused flooding. People walking across what they thought was firm snow would fall through into fast-running streams that hadn't even been there before. Luckily no one drowned but a few people got very wet!

Of course, water is a major problem at Low Birk Hatt because we have to go out to find it. We have never had water simply by turning on a tap like most people. Our supply comes from the stream which flows about forty yards from the front door, or from the barrel which collects the rainwater from the roof. In summer it's easy, but winter does present certain difficulties. Sometimes I have to dig a path through the snow down to the stream and use a pick on the frozen stream. Often it can take a little while to melt down the pieces of ice to make drinking water. Usually I keep two buckets full of water but that's no good in winter because they are plastic and will not stand the frost. Years ago we stored water in a big cream pot but that came to grief during a hard frost and we had to resort on one occasion to a possing tub – that is a fluted tub made from galvanized metal which was common to most households before washing machines – which, of course, had to be used for soaking the dirty clothes on washing day. This was when I was a girl and we had a lot of calves to feed and water.

On occasion there isn't sufficient water available from the stream or the rainwater tub, and I have to go down to the reservoir, which I call the Mississippi, to rinse the washing. In recent times I have been able to go down to the hostel, where my good friend Richard Megson gives me the opportunity to wash in lovely hot water. But it's a fair distance to walk there and it is, I suppose, a lot handier to pop down to the reservoir. I can have the washing done and back home again by the time I get to Richard's place.

To be honest I never get much washing done during the winter months. Usually it is done during the summer, certainly for my better clothes.

As for toilet facilities, I have an earth closet so the lack of water does not affect that side of things. Trouble is, the closet does get full and I have no means of cleaning it out. It's such an unpleasant job and I just cannot cope with it. In the old days people used to put ashes on top, but I prefer to use a utensil and I take it out on to the pasture. Not a thrilling subject to discuss, but it is the most practical method.

I suppose it will be the winters that will eventually finish my deep attachment to Low Birk Hatt, now that I am getting older. Two years ago, for example, I had a rough time. The weather became very bitter up here and because it had been a bad summer I had kept two of my cattle in the byre by the house all the time. This meant I had to get hay from the top barn for the rest of my cattle, which were still outside. So I dragged the sledge two fields up to the top byre, and the going was tough because of the molehills. And I had a slight mishap, the simplest thing in the world, really, when I was using a shovel in the calf house. I had a bullock, a nice quiet beast called Charlie, and I lost my grip on the shovel when he knocked into me. Unfortunately, the shaft went over the top of my foot and Charlie stood on it. It hurt a bit at the time, but I got myself free and didn't think a lot about it just then. I still had to get the hay down from the top byre to take to the cattle in the bottom byre on my sledge. Because of the pain I couldn't manage to pull the sledge in the uphill parts, so I had to break the bales in half, tie them up separately and carry them to the level bits, and load up again. It had been a very hard frost, the path was very slippery, and that night was particularly cold. My foot was giving me murder, and it got worse during the next few days, but I still had to go out and fodder the cattle. I didn't strap it up or anything like that – in fact, I did nothing with it. But it healed itself eventually. All in all it's an experience I would not like to repeat.

A BIRD'S-EYE VIEW OF BALDERSDALE

To appreciate properly the difference between a winter which the majority of people experience and the kind with which the people in the high Pennines have to cope, you need a bird's-eye view. It can be a revelation to fly by helicopter from the A1 at Scotch Corner, up the valley of the Tees towards the high country, when the temperatures fall and the skies become leaden. The fields around Barnard Castle can be quite green and pleasant, but a few miles further on you meet the snow line. From then on it becomes an arctic scene. Two or three miles out of Barnard Castle you can see a light covering of white – enough for pedestrians to consider galoshes but far short of a digging-out job with the shovel. But at the entrance to Baldersdale, the difference is dramatic. Here the land rises to a thousand feet or more above sea level. And just over the moors in a northerly direction is Birkdale, where the counties of Yorkshire, Durham and West-morland meet by a perpetually angry stream called Maize Beck and the hills soar to a deep-frozen two thousand feet.

When a flurry of snow lightly dusts the roads and pathways of the urban and suburban areas, you can be sure that Baldersdale and the rest of the high Pennines will be thigh-deep. When the research for *Too Long a Winter*, the first film documentary about Hannah, was being finalized around the end of October 1972, a certain hope was expressed about the weather. It would suit the purposes of the programme if there would be snow on the ground when the film unit arrived in November. The landlord of the Fox and Hounds in Cotherstone, which stands at the entrance of Baldersdale and was to become the front-line headquarters for the film makers, scoffed at this idea. He offered a complimentary bottle of wine if there was any significant snow around the pub when they arrived to commence filming in November. Came the day, and the film unit – a ponderous line of vehicles, carrying half a ton of exceedingly expensive equipment and all the people required to make it work efficiently – rumbled out of the centre of Leeds. The weather was benevolent for the time of the year. A few rain squalls, perhaps, but the temperature was well above freezing.

However, there was to be a significant change as the convoy journeyed further north. At Scotch Corner, the rain had changed colour. It was white and floated around. Five miles from Cotherstone it began to blow a blizzard. By the time the film crew arrived at the door of the Fox and Hounds, the drifts were rising to eighteen inches. Not a word was spoken as they made their way to the bar, but a well-chilled bottle of wine was uncorked and waiting . . .

The next two weeks will never be forgotten by all those who were privileged to work on *Too Long a Winter*. On one occasion a furious blizzard howled across a landscape illuminated by a sunset of bloodshot gold. Two men held out their sheepskin coats to shield the camera from the slanting snow; another lay full length in the drift to hold the tripod steady as Hannah led her white cow out of the storm and into the byre. It was a wondrous sequence, which would later move millions of viewers.

A few days later, the storm became so violent that

sheep became buried in six-foot drifts of snow, and the camera recorded farmers scrabbling down with their hands to release buried sheep, pinpointed by amazingly perceptive Border collies. The Yorkshire Television helicopter, which had lifted the crew in, landed in pitch darkness, totally against the ground rules laid down by the Civil Aviation Authority, and lifted out the film equipment. The pilot, who was as skilled as he was courageous, wisely refused to return to lift out the crew.

It was seven miles from that location to the nearest road, where the crew vehicles were parked. The route back had been totally covered by snow. Fortunately, the crew were not then aware that in recent recorded history three men had perished trying to walk the same route in midwinter. They had simply lost their way because the track was obliterated, and had wandered into oblivion – frozen to death. By 1972, presumably to guide people in the same predicament, posts five feet high had been driven into the ground beside the track. Along some stretches only eighteen inches were visible. But the way to safety was thus signposted. Some hours later – no one counted, but it was a long time – eight soaking, snow-covered individuals just – but only just – on the right side of hypothermia made it to the main Teesdale road, which snow-ploughs had kept open. They were amazed and delighted to find on that isolated junction the tiniest pub they had ever encountered, tucked away in a bend in the empty road. Fifteen people would have packed the place out. It was totally empty, and the landlord clearly expected no custom whatsoever that evening since he was re-clining in his private quarters. But he had lit a good coal fire in his bar. He probably thought it was the gale that blasted his door open, but for the next hour he was busy dispensing more whisky than he would normally expect to sell in a week. Or, perhaps, a month.

Every working moment of those two uncomfortable, exhausting, memorable weeks was lived on the ex-treme edge. The generator which tried to make it to Low Birk Hatt Farm, to provide camera lights, turned over on its side and had to be hauled out by tractor. After one session filming from a helicopter the camera-man's limbs were so stiff he was 'locked' into a sitting position and had to be carried to safety and warmth. Everyone suffered from that daily and prolonged exposure to a Baldersdale winter – swollen faces and aching joints were commonplace. Everyone, that is, except Hannah. She moved with a nunlike tranquillity from one sequence to the next, thinking nothing of being asked to drag a beast through a blizzard, and clearly suffering none of the discomfort felt by others. The elements may have seemed brutal to the docu-mentary makers (and some had roughed it in various parts of the world) but to someone like Hannah who had experienced the winters of 1947 and 1962 that November was child's play.

In between the exterior locations Hannah sat by the coal fire in her kitchen, and by the illumination cast by an oil lamp, as the camera turned, she described her incredibly spartan lifestyle. Living alone, with no electricity, no water on tap, one cow and a calf, and an income of £280 a year – 'if things go well'. Her expenditure on food for the month had edged up to £5! These provisions were left for collection by a local grocer on the dry-stone wall by the single road that winds through the dale, a long and difficult walk from Low Birk Hatt.

Essentially, Hannah was a castaway of life. An only child, all her relatives and close friends in Baldersdale had either died or moved away, and she became an abandoned person in a mostly abandoned dale. It is hard to imagine anyone else in this island who was more isolated and more materially deprived. Yet no resentment showed as she talked about her life and philosophy. Nor one jot of self-pity. Indeed, she seemed well content with her lot in life, and her face shone as she outlined her thoughts. She spoke in a curiously musical, richly accented way with a certain pattern that could only be described as antique – as though the speech mannerisms of the local Dalesfolk of two centuries ago had been preserved within Hannah. Clearly the lady could communicate. Everyone at Yorkshire Television conceded that as the film rushes were viewed, sequenced, edited and dubbed. But no one could have envisaged then with just what power.

Hannah's film was transmitted at 10.30 p.m. on Tuesday, 30 January 1973, to an audience approaching five million – a very respectable rating for a documentary shown at a time when most people are either retiring for the night or thinking about it.

The instant response was very favourable and next morning the reviews were superb. All the quality papers led with an assessment of *Too Long a Winter*, and marvelled at the astonishing life led by this old lady with the gleaming white hair in that frozen lonely Yorkshire dale. Old lady, indeed! She was only forty-six at the time, but sheer hardship and constant exposure to the worst elements the high Pennines could mete out had drained her youth away. It wasn't so much that she looked old and wrinkled (if you could discount the gleaming white halo of hair) since her complexion was as smooth and pink as an infant's. But she conveyed an impression of someone much older because her movements were restricted by rheumatism and her limbs made frail by lack of proper nourishment over the years.

On that first morning after transmission, none of the production team had the slightest idea of the impact the film – well, Hannah Hauxwell – had made on the general public. But it had started an avalanche.

The first intimation of its scope came when the producer of Yorkshire Television's daily regional current affairs programme, *Calendar*, came to complain bitterly that the task of getting that evening's show on the air had been seriously handicapped. The Yorkshire Television switchboard in Leeds with its myriad lines had been jammed all day with calls about Hannah. The London office reported a similar problem, and so did the YTV branches in Sheffield and Hull. All the other ITV companies throughout the land coped with their own flood of interest. It continued unabated for two days, and the gallant switchboard operators were near exhaustion. Fortunately, most of them had seen the programme and were committed admirers of Hannah.

Then came the mail. The GPO in Leeds rang to say it would have to make special arrangements to cope with the volume, and delivered bulging sacks direct to the production team. The general tenor of the letters, the thread that ran through the vast majority, soon became clear. The correspondents expressed deep gratitude to Hannah – they were so inspired by her sublimely tranquil and uncomplaining acceptance of the kind of material deprivation considered unacceptable by modern society, so moved by her angelic demeanour and indomitable spirit, that they had been obliged to consider their own situation, and concluded that their individual complaints about life were so paltry by comparison that their entire perspective had been changed. Most enclosed a gift – 'please, please accept it, Hannah – I feel I owe you such a lot' – ranging from cheques up to one hundred pounds from people one hoped could afford it, down to postal orders for fifty pence from pensioners. Cash, too, in all denominations – and then the parcels followed, clothes, food, presents of all kinds.

The Press leapt on to the story. They realized a new star had emerged and a most unusual one at that. Photographers arrived to take pictures of the mail bags, and the Yorkshire TV still of Hannah inhabited the front pages for weeks.

The stunned production team were dealing with the tidal wave as best they could when an awful realization dawned. What had they done to this woman? Completely ruined her life? A team was dispatched immediately to Baldersdale and discovered a remarkable scene. The lanes in the dale were full of people trying to locate Hannah, some in caravans. Fortunately, the isolation of Low Birk Hatt is its own security so Hannah was spared the arrival of a regiment. The few who did get through, mostly mature if determined ladies carrying packets of tea, butter and biscuits, did not create any serious inconvenience. It transpired that Hannah was well capable of coping with this sudden celebrity status, displaying a curiously ingenuous confidence as in later months she met people ranging from royalty to hard-nosed journalists, and completely disarmed them all.

Only the money pouring in by every post seriously concerned her. At first she declined to accept it, wanting it sent back. She was persuaded to concede on that point, then proposed to share everything with the production team – until it was pointed out that if just one penny, or a single biscuit, was diverted in that direction, and it became known, we'd be lynched.

Hannah's film had a dramatic effect wherever it was shown, and won a clutch of awards. Gifts and visitors came from all over the English-speaking world as television stations overseas, alerted by all the publicity, snapped up transmission rights. A group from Switzerland turned up on the doorstep of Low Birk Hatt on her birthday (they knew – they had gifts), a whole cheese arrived overland from New Zealand, and the rooms at the farm began to fill up. Perhaps the most confused man in the Yorkshire Dales during the first frantic days after the first transmission was the Baldersdale postman. If anyone ever deserved a hardship bonus, it was him. The people at the GPO were also remarkably efficient, since letters addressed as vaguely as 'The Old Lady in the TV Programme, Somewhere in the Yorkshire Dales' were faithfully delivered.

It seemed that half the world wanted to give Hannah something and a classic example occurred when the programme was shown by a Dutch television station. When a senior executive arrived at the studio a day or two later he found parcels piling up in the reception area. He telephoned Yorkshire Television to seek explanations and advice, demanding plaintively in a guttural accent: 'Who the hell is this Hannah Hauxvell?'

The complete answer to that question, one suspects, will never satisfactorily be answered. Certainly she rarely fails to surprise as she faces up serenely to various situations which would disorientate people with much more sophistication. For instance, when the Yorkshire Television helicopter landed on her doorstep for the first time, it was feared that the experience may be alarming to her, something akin to an alien spaceship settling on to the average suburban lawn. Not a bit of it. Within minutes Hannah was alongside the aircraft examining it closely, and touching it with her fingertips, as if to make sure it was real.

The offer of a quick flight was accepted without a moment's hesitation and she was whisked away to join the gulls that swoop around the reservoir and over her roof. 'Now that's what I call a real bird's-eye view!' she exclaimed as she landed, beaming with delight.

There was another memorable moment a few months later when she was flown to Leeds by the same helicopter – 'I have to admit, it's my favourite method of transport' – to attend a Press conference. It was her first visit to a city and she was taken aback by the volume of traffic – 'I had heard about this kind of thing, but it's quite frightening close to like this,' she said, as she stood on the pavement in City Square and watched four lanes of vehicles jousting strenuously for position. The roar of the traffic was almost drowned by a furious burst of camera shutters as the assembled Press took their first opportunity of photographing Hannah in an urban situation.

The incident which will stick for ever in the minds of those who witnessed it came when she was being ushered into the main entrance of Yorkshire Television. As she came face to face with the revolving doors her escorts stood aside to allow her to precede. But Hannah did not move, merely studied the revolving doors with interest. She showed no inclination whatsoever to go forward. Then it suddenly occurred to one of the party that these must be the first set of revolving doors Hannah had ever encountered, so he leaned forward and set them moving. 'Oh,' said Hannah, with that familiar beam; 'my goodness, what a clever idea,' and entered the building.

Many incidents of a similarly charming nature were to follow as the years went by, without any diminution in the public fascination with this spinster lady from a remote Yorkshire dale dressed in complex layers of well-laundered rags. Speaking engagements, regular television and radio appearances, countless newspaper interviews, a second major network documentary, have had no effect whatsoever on her personality and character.

She enjoys these diversions, is human enough to relish all the attention, and the material benefits were not only welcome but essential for her well-being. But diversions are all they are, and ever will be . . . not central to life. For Hannah there can only be one important base – Low Birk Hatt Farm, Baldersdale.

One day, illness, or the realization that she no longer possesses the strength to cope with the unremitting hardships of a stock farm and the 365-days-a-year toil, will force her to leave.

In the meantime, as she so sweetly says, through her tears, to those who have over many years tried gently to persuade her to go straight away and live the rest of her life in comfort: 'You are right, of course, but you see . . . I'm in chains to this place.'

FOUR

Dreams of Romance

There are few things in the human condition more likely to create intrigue and speculation than the person who manages to progress through life without marrying, and those who have avoided a close relationship of any kind with the opposite sex arouse special interest. Hannah never married and never had a close relationship, but she had her dreams. When she was maturing into young womanhood Baldersdale was well populated with youngsters of equivalent age – that is to say, eligible for Hannah. Photographs indicate that she was a bonny young lass likely to stir the emotions of any number of local young men. There was also no lack of opportunity to meet up with your contemporaries in and around the dale – there was even a dance hall of a kind.

Oh yes, it was at the Strathmore Arms at Hury, and we called it the Show Room, and sometimes the Hut. It was in the field behind the Strathmore Arms, actually. It was built of wood and it fairly shook during some of the more energetic dances, like the Lancers. The place was used for all sorts of important occasions and I can remember walking down there to celebrate King George V and Queen Mary's Silver Jubilee. I was so proud that day because it was the first time I wore a rather special red coat with matching red hat. It wasn't new, of course, but made of a very good material. I was also given a Jubilee mug at school, which I still have.

The first dance band at the Show Room was made up of people in the dale and they called themselves the Arcadians. Joe Donald played the drums and William and Nellie Addison, who were brother and sister, played violin and piano. Nellie was very good and a natural musician who could play without looking at the piano, which meant she could watch the dancing at the same time. The band platform was very small and cramped, so much so that an overenthusiastic violinist could place the others at some risk from a poke in the eye from his bow.

Occasionally we would be treated to performances by visiting groups who had actually broadcast on the wireless, such as the Bainbridge Brothers, Lance and Jack, and the Swaledale Singers, who sang a varied programme of real life and beauty but created something of a problem with their final number. They chose 'In the Sweet Bye and Bye', which is a Methodist hymn, and this upset a High Church person in the audience. We had our own talent in Baldersdale, of course, including a relative of mine, Norman Bayles, who had a very nice tenor voice. Whenever I hear the song 'Moonlight and Roses' I think of him because that was his favourite.

We would have visiting bands for the dances, too, and I remember one called The Five Aces who came from Copley and were very good. The favourite dances were the good old ones like the military two-step, the Eva three-step, the valeta and the St Bernard waltz. Not that I danced very much. In fact you could say that I was a real wallflower. You see, people tended to stay in groups, very clannish you could say, and I didn't belong to any of them. Maybe I'm being unkind, but they weren't too friendly, didn't shout out 'Haway, come on . . . thou might as well join us,' as one would have wished. They seemed to dance all the time with their own group of friends or relatives. In fact, out of all the times I went to the Show Room I was only asked to dance twice.

Then matters were made worse by Uncle's attitude. He was the man of the house, you see, since my father was dead, and he became very strict when I was around fourteen or fifteen. One night I stopped on a bit at the dance in Cotherstone and had to walk home because I couldn't get a lift from anyone. You didn't see many cars in those days and most people biked or walked. It took two hours, even using all the short cuts, to walk to Low Birk Hatt, and it was about 1 a.m. when I got back. Uncle waited up for me and was so cross that I was really frightened. So that put an end to that . . . no more dances down at Cotherstone for me.

I was very annoyed and upset at the time because there were other girls of my age in the dale and they could go and I could not. It seemed so unfair but perhaps he was right. The other girls went together in a group but I was on my own, and I suppose someone could have followed me from the dance . . . I hadn't a clue about such things in those days.

So I consequently never really learned to dance because of the limited opportunities. Mind, there was one night that I've often thought about. It was rather special, and perhaps I shouldn't mention it . . . because it was just one of those wartime things. I met him at a dance, a nice soldier who was playing double bass in the band. He had light hair, corn colour, and it was very curly. From the south of the country he was, and stationed at Cotherstone.

He asked me to dance but I said I couldn't. He wasn't put off and said that if I would please stay he would dance every dance with me. But it was something of a Cinderella situation – I had to get home early or risk another hot reception from Uncle.

It was a nice happening . . . a sweet memory. Just to

think, he said he would dance *every* dance with me if only I would stay. But I never saw him again. Often I've wondered what happened to him, whether or not he survived the war. I can still hear the tune he played in the band after we talked – 'Ain't She Sweet' – and it will always remind me of him.

No, I'm afraid I've never really had what you could call a boyfriend, someone to come calling to take me out. Of course, I had my dreams, like all young girls, of a tall, dark and handsome man coming striding over the fell one day to claim me as his own. And I used to swallow up all those stories in the women's magazines, which were very kindly saved for me by two ladies down the dale. There were romantic books too, such as *A Mad Love* by Charlotte M. Graham, and *East Lynne*, which I think is a great, great book. Another beautiful volume was *The Rosary* by Florence M. Barclay which is a story intertwined with a song which I heard once on a record sung by Paul Robeson. I've read lots of books, including several of the classics, but haven't liked some of the authors some dote on, like Jane Austen and the Brontës. I considered that the story of the Brontës themselves is more interesting than some of the characters and situations they wrote about. I've only read *Wuthering Heights* of theirs, as it happens, and I wasn't too keen on parts of that. I thought that Heathcliff had no redeeming features at all. I know that some ladies think it so romantic, the meeting on the moors with Heathcliff and everything. But they are welcome to him. I wouldn't have gone to meet him under any circumstances.

Oddly enough I never met anyone I thought I might like to marry when I was younger, in my teens and early twenties. It was much later on in my thirties and on one occasion even later than that, when I met two men who at different times became very special to me. But it was just my foolishness – I am sure neither ever felt that way about me. They both retained a certain affection for me but not in the way I wanted.

It wouldn't have worked out with the first gentleman, as it happens, because although he had a lovely smile he was a ladies' man and he did like drink too much. I think he had a little corner in his heart for me but if we had got together and he had gone off with someone else I couldn't have stood the hurt and humiliation.

Anyhow he went away and met the lady who became his wife in London, I believe, and they had a child. We still remained good friends.

Now the other gentleman I liked very much. I was in my forties when I met him – call it middle-aged madness if you like, but he was so kind and thoughtful. It wasn't as though either of these men had led me to expect anything, gave me anything to hope for, it's just that I really liked them, particularly the one I encountered later on. He got married a year or two later and had a son and a daughter. Funnily enough – now this makes me think a bit, although it was probably just because he liked the name – he did call his daughter Hannah.

Oh yes! I've had my dreams, and I do feel that, if you have never had a close relationship with somebody, something in you dries up . . . goes dead, one might say. They say that machinery works better when in use. But if I had been given the chance when I was younger I might easily have made a mistake and gone for good looks and he might have turned out to be Old Nick to live with. Since getting older I've sometimes hoped for someone with whom to have a good relationship. Not to marry, but just to meet up on a regular basis and do nice things together such as walks, long discussions about books and music, that sort of thing.

There are some people who have a remarkable ability to attract the opposite sex, and sometimes it *is* sex that it's all about. But I think that sex can be a fleeting thing and sometimes I believe that if it is that alone as the basis of a relationship, then all the finer and better qualities are thrown out of the window. Personally, I do not think that sex is important, but if there is someone you like, and share affection, interest, respect and trust, then perhaps sex can mix in a little. But I put it at the bottom of the list and consider it can really be done without. And then, of course, it becomes less important as the years go by – that's one of the compensations of getting older.

On the same subject, I suppose I have to point out that I have never really wanted to have children. I have never liked babies, and I am not really comfortable with them when they get older. That is not to say that I haven't met some canny little folk, but generally I don't speak their language because I have never been used to them. I realize there are some women, and I know one or two in Baldersdale, who cannot resist babies and go all to pieces whenever they meet one, whereas I am the same with dogs. I'm just daft about dogs.

Under the circumstances then, perhaps it was wisely ordered that I never found a man to form that special relationship. But I have sometimes thought there might be a problem in the afterlife, if there is such a thing – one hopes but I am not convinced – when one is supposed to be reunited with one's loved ones. I have been to funerals in Baldersdale where bereaved people have shown supreme faith, being convinced that death is only a temporary thing and that they would meet up with their loved ones again.

So maybe I will lose out a little in the romantic sense

when it comes to my turn. Of course, one hopes to meet one's parents and other dear relatives, but there won't be someone special to me.

And now it seems that I will go to my grave without meeting that special person.

FIVE

My Music . . . the Talented Tallentires and a Poetic Grandad

Hannah's apparent simplicity and innate modesty cloaks many talents. One night during the making of the first film in November 1972, she dusted down a piece of furniture in that crowded kitchen of hers (which everyone had supposed to be a writing desk), lifted the lid and revealed . . . a miniature organ! Hannah explained that it was one of the elegant gifts that her mother had brought down when she was given in marriage to her half-cousin (on the Tallentire side of the family), William Bayles Hauxwell. The film crew gathered around to admire this splendid piece of furniture, clearly an antique of considerable interest, possibly value – if it was in good order and free of worm and rot. Did it still work? Hannah smiled, pulled out a stool (which had seen better days) and began to play. She had never mentioned that she possessed musical ability, so the crew listened spellbound for a few minutes as she played the carol 'Silent Night, Holy Night', as though she had been rehearsing for a month. In reality, she hadn't touched it in years. Instinctively her audience came out of their bemused state and worked quickly. The lights were swung round, the Nagra tape recorder switched on and the camera hastily placed on its tripod and pointed. The result was another memorable moment in *Too Long a Winter*. Still clad in her tattered working clothes, her wellingtons pumped away assiduously to give the instrument the breath it required. It turned out that Hannah had inherited a natural gift for music.

I did have a few lessons, with a lady down the dale called Annie Bayles. She lived at New Houses, and was related to me in a mixed-up kind of way – her father and my grandmother were cousins, but what that made me to Miss Bayles I cannot imagine! It was the year before war broke out in 1939 and a small sum was paid for a quarter's lessons, thirteen in all, I think, but I did miss one or two. Mother was a grand player, of course . . . much better than I ever was . . . but she thought I might do better if someone else taught me, and she was such a busy person with all those old people to care for and Daddy ailing like he was.

It turned out to be a lot easier than I thought because I was scarcely quick on the uptake when it came to lessons. But I found I could just sit down and play by ear. I do not claim to be gifted – it's just something you either possess or you don't. I must say it was a great relief not to have to try to understand it all from books.

Mother would play really good music at home, and I still have her books of music – Beethoven, Chopin and Tchaikovsky. It was lovely to listen to, one of the treasured memories of my childhood, in fact. But as times became more difficult with the passing years I suppose she had neither the time nor the inclination to play music.

Mother was a Tallentire and it was that side of the family which had the interest in music and . . . well, talent, I suppose, like the first part of their name. They were rather better off than most, I think, and they owned an inn called New Spittal, between Bowes and Brough, over to the west. I believe it may be the Bowes Moor Hotel now, which I hear is quite a large and important establishment and in a very good position on the main road to the M6.

They had a variety of musical instruments, including violins, and my grandfather Tallentire created quite a stir locally in later years by travelling all the way to Manchester to hear the Brothers Hamburg play. I cannot imagine how on earth he even came to know about them because it was long before radio was introduced. Anyway, they were called Mark and Jean, pronounced in the French manner. One played the piano and the other the violin and they were quite celebrated. Grandfather's principal interest was to hear the one who played the piano but when he got there he was rather taken up with the violinist. He could play both instruments himself.

The entire family seemed to be steeped in music and I understand that when a new harmonium was introduced in Spittal Chapel there was keen interest in comparing that with the one they owned – such as whether one had more stops than the other.

Obviously the younger members of the family became too enthusiastic about it all because Grandfather Tallentire threatened a different kind of stop if they carried on spending so much of their time playing and talking about music. He thought, perhaps, that not enough attention was being paid to work. Indeed, he had, in fact, smashed one of their violins when he lost his temper for the same reason in the previous year.

Of course, most people around here relied on Chapel for their music, and very good it was too. The Tallentires were staunch Chapel folk even though they owned a pub. I am not sure how they reconciled that situation, since the Methodists were very much against alcoholic drink. I am not sure about the precise details, but I do believe that when Great-Grandfather Tallentire

Grandmother Hauxwell and Uncle Thomas Tallentire Hauxwell, who lived with Hannah

Buttermaking at Cotherstone (Beamish)

Sweeping hay at New Homes, Baldersdale, 1938 (Beamish)

Hury Show, Baldersdale (Beamish, North of England Open Air Museum)

Sheep shearing in Baldersdale

Sheep dipping at West Birk Hatt. Left to right: Sam Fawcett; Tom Fawcett, Sam's bachelor brother; George Fawcett; and Hannah's uncle Thomas Hauxwell

Above
Grandfather James
and Grandmother
Hauxwell

Right
Sam Fawcett

Opposite page
Hannah's mother
as a young woman

Hannah as a
teenager with her
mother

Haytime at West
Park, Cotherstone
(Beamish)

Baldersdale school
with Mrs Archer

John Thwaites with
Luther and Ruben
Tunstace

Hannah finds a quiet corner during the auction of her belongings
(Press Association)

became old and decided to retire he refused to allow his sons to carry on the licence.

Anyway, the Tallentires never gave up their music because when Grandfather Tallentire set up house in a little farm called North Side he went to buy an organ but took a fancy to a piano and came back with that instead. He was the one who went to hear the Brothers Hamburg.

Mother carried on the tradition in our house and she was a talented musician. I am sorry to say that I never heard her at her best because of circumstances.

Now, on the Hauxwell side I had a grandad to whom words were music. He played a very happy part in my childhood and just the thought of him makes me smile even today. James was his name, and he had a wonderful way with a poem or a recitation, and could remember dozens of really stirring examples. He came to Baldersdale a hundred years or so ago to help construct the Hury Reservoir – I think Low Birk Hatt was built around the same time. He was born around the Darlington area and I heard that his family once had money, but lost it in some way. Mind, he was rather a wild card was Granda, rather too fond of strong drink. He would often go down to the Hare and Hounds at the west end of Hury – it's gone now, of course – but he was a grand man and his scarum ways did not alter my affection for him one bit. Granda's fondness for alcohol is one of the reasons why I have never touched it in my life . . . although I do admit to having some rum sauce once. But no, I do not want to take the chance myself in case it turns out to be a family weakness.

When they were younger he and Grandma had a little farm and I think that Grandma did not have an easy life with him and had to do a good bit of the farmwork. She was also a grand needlewoman, a talent which rather curiously led to a change in her religious affiliations. Ever since the Wesleys brought their message into the western dales, Methodism had been the strongest religion around here and we had a nice little chapel in the dale. The Church of England hadn't a place of their own and were obliged to use a room in the schoolhouse for their services on Sundays. The school was connected with the Church in some way, although it had been built by Dalesfolk with dales money. Anyway, the clergyman who came to look after those who were C of E got to know about Grandma's skill as a sewer and also knew that a little bit of extra money would be welcome in her household. So he arranged a job as a sewing teacher at the school for her. I suppose she was so grateful that she became one of his flock. But her daughter-in-law, my mother, stayed with the Methodists. As for me, I went to both establishments as a girl – Sunday School in the afternoon at the church and evening service at the chapel.

I must say that the Methodists had the edge when it came to music and poetry, and Granda used to encourage me to take part. Chapel Anniversary was always a treat and one year I sang a song, 'Won't You Buy My Pretty Flowers?'. Then I would do a recitation, sometimes one of Granda's favourites like 'The Arab's Farewell to his Steed'. I can still remember most of the words to this day:

> *My Beautiful, my Beautiful,*
>   *that stands so meekly by*
> *His proudly arched and glossy neck*
>   *and dark and fiery eye.*
> *Stranger hath thy bridle rein,*
>   *thy master hath his gold . . .*

And of course it all ends happily when the Arab obviously cannot bear to part with his horse:

> *Who said that I had given thee up?*
>   *Who said that thou were sold?*
> *Tis false, tis false, my Arab steed,*
>   *I fling them back their gold.*
> *Thus I leap upon thy back*
>   *And scour the distant plains;*
> *Away, who o'er takes us now*
>   *May claim thee for his pains.*

Oh, how I do like those lines, and when I repeat them now it brings back so many happy memories of that scamp of a grandfather of mine.

SIX

Festive Times . . . and Funerals

People who live, work, play and die in the more remote rural places like Baldersdale are distanced from the rest of us, and not just in the geographic sense. Their lives have a totally separate base, their vital points of reference are distinctly different from the majority who dwell in the more materially blessed urban areas. There, one is largely protected from the extremities of nature. But in the higher reaches of the Yorkshire Dales, there is nowhere to hide. The forces of nature, even today, are in control, and a winter storm which will inconvenience town and city dwellers can still devastate the hopes and aspirations and the economic structure of a Dales community. When Hannah was young and in her formative years, this dichotomy was even more pronounced. The difference is essentially one of the spirit and it manifests itself in the habits and attitudes of country folk. Stoicism replaces sentimentality, pragmatism is preferred to romance, and the need to survive from one season to the next overrides everything. Hannah Hauxwell possesses an unusual sensitivity for one who was reared to the truly spartan life of an isolated dale in the thirties and forties when sheer hardship invariably deadened any aesthetic tendencies. It was a community which was lagging behind the lowlands by at least a century. Electricity and water on tap were unattainable dreams for most, but then, nobody had much time to indulge in dreams. Every day of the week, fifty-two weeks of the year, the toil was relentless. Cows to be milked twice a day, every day, water to be carried to all the cattle, fodder to drag to the high pastures, hay to be cut if the weather was benevolent, dry-stone walls to be repaired after the ravages of winter, cows to be calved and ewes to be lambed (usually in the middle of the night), horses to harness, drains to be dug . . . the list is endless. It is truly remarkable that, given the scant time for leisure, a fine appreciation of music and literature existed in certain isolated pockets of Baldersdale which Hannah was privileged to enjoy. And Chapel was uniformly well supported because of the unswerving belief of people who live in this way that some enormous, inexplicable force shapes their destiny. The hours spent in this manner would have to be paid back, though, usually at the cost of sleep.

The women of Baldersdale, as in all similar communities, went with their men into the fields and byres and worked shoulder to shoulder. They were excused few, if any, tasks. Hannah may appear to be a frail pensioner but a lifetime's exposure to the hard labour of rural life enables her to endure the most extreme elements far better than urban-reared people half her age.

The women, too, had to cope with all the household duties, including feeding men and hired hands with appetites honed by constant fresh air and exercise, with none of the labour-saving aids which most women took for granted. Naturally, Hannah had to take her place on the Baldersdale treadmill, working to the orders of her uncle in the fields (her father died when she was an infant) and assisting her mother in the kitchen and wash house. In some ways she was very unsuited to this life – indeed, she has described herself as a 'misfit' in Baldersdale. Despite her bleak background and threadbare, Dickensian sartorial habits, she certainly transmits an aura of elegance and gentility. Her delicate mannerisms and overall maidenly demeanour suggest that she would be much better suited, say, in the tearooms of Cheltenham or Bath, with life revolving around the quieter charitable events, bridge parties and chamber music. This gives the impression that a tiny error has been made in the Grand Design.

Hannah is, for instance, sentimental about animals,

not a common trait among Dalesfolk since it is counterproductive in a society geared to the continual slaughter and selling of cattle, sheep and pigs. She became aware at an early stage that there was an entirely different way of life available not far outside Baldersdale, perhaps more appealing to her, but it could have been on another planet.

Hannah clearly possesses a unique quality which gives her a remarkable perspective of the very fabric of Baldersdale. She may perhaps have felt a little out of place but she articulates a rare understanding of what was going on in the place, all underpinned by an almost total recall of the fascinating minutiae of day-to-day events. When it came to the major events in the life of that other world outside Baldersdale, such as Christmas, the celebrations were muted, to say the least.

At Low Birk Hatt we didn't have Christmases in the generally accepted sense. Mother had so much to do outside and the old folk living with us were ailing and needed a lot of attention.

Christmas dinner rather depended on the weather. If it was stormy people were too busy looking after the farm and the animals to bother much, but when it was clear we had a nice meal. Once we had a goose but Mother was so ill that she had to go to bed after she had roasted it. I was told that before she got married and went into farming she lived with a great-aunt and enjoyed a good meal every day. A different way of life altogether.

Nor did we make much fuss over presents. Mother did once give me a tin of toffees, all wrapped in gold paper, which was a special treat – I still have the pretty tin, all pink, red and gold. I would get a stocking with a few bits of things in when I was young and Grandma used to make a big cake with white icing, but that would be when Daddy was alive. But school was a different thing at Christmas, and very nice too. We were given crêpe paper to make hats, lanterns and crackers, and Mrs Archer would provide us with a sweet or a nut to put in the cracker. Then we decorated the school ready for a really splendid children's tea in the afternoon, which was usually followed by a lantern slide show in the evening for the parents, also very enjoyable. It was always a bit dull and unwelcome coming back home to Low Birk Hatt afterwards.

Strange to say, I didn't really like carol singers. There was something rather eerie about people turning up unexpectedly around the door and starting to sing. When I was small I would creep into a corner. I suppose the best Christmases I knew happened over at Clove Lodge where Mr and Mrs Atkinson and the

Misses Hind would always make a special thing of it. They had a juniper bush which was placed in the hub of a cart wheel covered in crêpe paper. We would decorate it with pieces of cotton wool for snow, and one or two other nice things like those shining coloured balls, which seemed to be metallic, but which were easily broken.

But Christmas at home was very quiet. We didn't invite friends with Mother being placed as she was, but if neighbours called they would be offered a glass of something, usually homemade ginger cordial, and a bit of cake if we had it. We didn't have parties, nor did we celebrate my birthday as most children do. Uncle wanted me to have a twenty-first party but 1 August is an inconvenient date because it's usually in the middle of haytiming, so we didn't bother.

One Christmas, Mother managed to find the time to make me a dolly, but only because I pestered. Maybe I was being a bit greedy because I already had the one I have mentioned before made by Mrs Fawcett from West Birk Hatt. But Mother must have known how precious dollies were to me and set about making me a black one taking the pattern from my old one, which I called Cuddles. She used an old black quilted petticoat and found some furry black fabric to use for its head and feet. Now, that was a really special present.

When I look back I realize just what a hard time Mother must have had because she did not enjoy what one might describe as robust health. In fact she became ill soon after I was born. She got out of bed too early, so the story goes, because there was so much washing piling up belonging to all the family, as well as me. Anyway, Mother became very ill with pleurisy and my father had to poultice her.

We never did have a proper wash house at our place like some people, with a big boiler and a fire underneath for hot water. Nor did we have sinks and drains, so all the water had to be carried in and carried out again when it was dirty.

I still have the big iron mangle she used to wring out the clothes. We didn't even have liquid or powders then, just Sunlight soap, which Mother cut into pieces and dissolved in a large iron pan on the fire. Then it would be mixed with the hot water in a possing tub, which was made from wood in the early days, but eventually we acquired a zinc one. The clothes were agitated by hand, using a wooden dolly, which had four short legs and a long handle.

Mother did all the cooking as well, and there was a problem in that department too because our oven was going home – that is to say, it was on its last legs – even before the war. But Mother did the best she could and made rabbit pies, apple pies, and obtained a very good recipe from Mrs Fawcett for a tattie cake, which was a bit like a Cornish pasty, without the meat, and a whole lot bigger. There were cakes and custards and homemade bread and teacakes, when people brought us fresh yeast from Barnard Castle. Mother was really a good cook but that oven was not exactly reliable – indeed, I do not know how she managed to get such nice things out of it.

We had a garden where vegetables and fruit grew very well. Grandad was the gardener and planted a lot of fruit trees, including gooseberry, blackcurrant, plum and loganberry for the jam-making. We even had a walnut tree which is still going, but it does not bear fruit any more. He was also very fond of flowers, and as well as things such as marigolds, pansies, marguerites and wallflowers, he grew a rose one doesn't see these days, which was very white when it first came out and then developed a lovely flush of pink. And it had a lovely perfume. So did the Southernwood which was a feathery blue-green plant – that's another plant I've never come across since, although I have to confess that I haven't seen many gardens. Grandma would use it for her buttonholes when she went to church, along with a flower or two.

I've heard say that Grandad used to rise at five o'clock in the morning during summertime to water the garden, all carried by hand, of course. He was so proud of it, and rightly so. But when Grandma died he just lost all interest in the garden and, since no one had the time to take it on, it became neglected. The nettles took over and nothing survives now.

It was such a shame because Grandad James Hauxwell had lived a life somewhat fuller and more exciting than most in Baldersdale. I understand he was always ready for a bit of mischief and they used to tell many tales about him. He had two brothers, one called Robert, who was employed in the household of the Duke and Duchess of Northumberland as a footman, I believe, and another called Frank who became a policeman. They were both very smart and correct, but Grandad was a little more wayward. He joined the Army – twice! First time his parents bought him out, but then he went and signed on again. He went down country with the Army, and there's a big difference between there and up here – it's not a place where economy is considered in the same way, so maybe he learned some bad habits, such as a tendency to alcoholic drink. Of course he acquired some better habits, such as that great liking for poetry and music.

Anyhow he came back to farming after leaving the Army. When he was young he used to live in a place called Manfield, near Darlington, along with his brother. Incidentally, the one who worked as a footman had to leave his job in order to get married to a girl who was also in service at the Duke's place. Apparently matrimony was not permitted for the servants.

Grandad went to work for a farmer who was rather an old skinflint. Another young man was in service there too, but he was from a rather well-to-do family who had paid the old man to teach their son the tricks of the trade. But he was granted no special treatment and had to toil just as hard as the hired hands. In fact, the farmer was so mean to this young man he determined to exact revenge. So when threshing time came round he bought a considerable amount of liquor which he concealed in strategic places.

Well, before mid-afternoon all the men – and extra help always came in for the threshing – were incapable of working. I daresay that Grandad enjoyed that because there is no doubt that he was fond of a drink. He could get up to all sorts of tricks and I was told that when another one of the lads at the same farm applied for a job as a coachman, Grandad gave him a reference. He had a lovely hand, and wrote about him that 'this man has been my coachman for a number of years and I have no hesitation in highly recommending him . . .'

Goodness knows how he signed himself, but I do believe it worked, and the lad got the job.

Grandad arrived in Baldersdale around the turn of the century, to work on the building of the reservoir, and came to lodge at Low Birk Hatt, when Great-Grandfather Tallentire was running it. It seems that other young men came to stay too – I suppose it must have been a very welcome extra source of income – and I understand that Great-Grandmother Tallentire was criticized for allowing young men to stay in the house when she had daughters. I do believe that came about because of an incident for which Grandfather Haux-well was responsible. You see, Great-Aunt Jane was a skilled dressmaker and made clothes for quite a number of young ladies in Baldersdale, and it was usual for them to try on the new clothes and have the final fittings in the kitchen. It seems that Grandfather either found, or perhaps made, a hole in the floorboards. And I'm afraid the young men used to use it as a peephole whilst the young ladies were in a state of undress. Eventually they were found out, and you can just imagine what a fuss that caused, all those years ago when Victoria was on the throne, and even the sight of a petticoat was forbidden to young men.

Yes, Grandad was something of a harum-scarum but I loved him nevertheless. I think his experience of farming was somewhat limited because of the time he had spent in the Army, and that would not make things easy for Grandma Hauxwell because she had to take on more responsibility around the farm. Perhaps because of his liking for drink, Grandmother would have to be the overseer, and do a good bit of the work herself. But Grandad did have certain very useful talents. He was particularly skilled with animals and he knew something about veterinary work, which came in very handy when any of the animals took ill, also during lambing and calving time. Horses were his speciality, and although he was rather a stout and shortish man – he sported a moustache – he was quite strong.

The passing years took their toll, of course, and he did go into a decline when Grandmother died. Because of the unusually large number of old folk living at Low Birk Hatt we had more than our share of funerals and everything was made worse when Daddy died at such a young age. He was only thirty-six and I was too young to remember much about it. He started with pleurisy which turned into pneumonia and because he wasn't a strong man it carried him off. I used to sleep in the same bed as my mother and father because of the shortage of space, but one morning I woke up in another room and I looked out and saw the undertaker standing at the top of the stairs.

Hannah, Barry Cockcroft and tape recorder
(*Overleaf*) Hannah with friends

(*Top*) Hannah and some of her belongings
(*Above*) Hannah asleep in her four poster bed and (*left*) her kitchen window – view slightly impeded

(*Top*) Winter in Baldersdale (*Above*) Hannah feeding the cattle and (*left*) at the door of Low Birk Hatt

(*Top*) Low Birk Hatt; Barry Cockcroft (in sheepskin jacket)
(*Above*) Hannah with her dog Timmy

(*Top*) Hannah with Ashley Jackson, celebrated Yorkshire artist; and Ashley Jackson's view of Low Birk Hatt

Funerals are very special occasions in the Dales, when people who may not be on the friendliest of terms would forget their differences for a while and come and pay their respects. Most everybody turned out, whoever it was. There was a custom called bidding, when the family of the deceased person would have cards printed to send round the dale. The relatives never delivered the cards themselves, but would choose a group of friends or neighbours. Some would take them to the top half of the dale, and the others the bottom half. In that way people were bidden to the funeral. The post would only be used for people who lived out of the dale. I still have all the cards to this day.

I was only a little girl when I went to my first funeral. Grandmother Hauxwell took me when her brother, John Bayles, died. Mind, I stayed at the house and didn't have to go to the graveside, but I can still see the procession of people.

Some came on foot, and others on horseback, or horse and trap. The coffin was carried on a horse-drawn cart because it was a long time before a motor hearse became available. Most people wore black and those who couldn't afford dark clothing managed to borrow some, and the men wore hard hats.

Daddy went to his grave at Romaldkirk in the same way, on our cart which was pulled by his favourite horse, a little cob called Dick. On occasion, so many people turned up to a Baldersdale funeral and the church or chapel became so crowded that people had to stand outside. I recall having to stand out in the cold at Cotherstone Chapel when one gentleman belonging to a family which had been in the dale for several generations was laid to rest. He was from the south side of the dale, which by custom went to Cotherstone, whilst we on our side went to Romaldkirk. There is no burial ground in Baldersdale itself.

I do not remember much about my father – just odd memories, like when he would lift me up on his horse and give me a ride. And when he would arrive from Barnard Castle with a heavy load of shopping on a bicycle and give me a nice round bun he would buy as a special treat from a shop called Guy's. He was a very serious man, I'm told, and totally unlike my uncle, his brother, who came to live with us and run the farm when father died. Grandma used to say they were like chalk and cheese, and that they should have been shaken up together in a bag to get more of a mixture. Then both might have been more sensible. Uncle was much more the happy-go-lucky extrovert whereas Daddy was shy and reserved, but that may have been due in part, at least, to the burdens he carried. He worked all hours, day and night, and in all weathers. I do know that at Low Birk Hatt, after finishing working in the fields all day, he would set to joinering at night, and made several of the doors and gates. I daresay he might have appeared more cheerful if his responsibilities had not been so heavy. You see, quite apart from all the work, he had such financial problems, particularly with the large mortgage on the farm.

With Uncle's help we all struggled on after he died, and when I got a bit older and left school it was not possible for me to contemplate leaving home to find a job and a new life outside Baldersdale. I was needed at Low Birk Hatt. You see, Mother was very subject to bad colds and influenza, even when she was young. She was no giver-in, but sometimes she got very high temperatures and just had to stay in bed. As for Uncle, he had suffered from rheumatism for as long as I can remember, so, all in all, we always had more work than we could really cope with. So I didn't have the same opportunities as other young people in the post-war years.

The very worst time came when Mother really took ill. The doctor sent her to hospital where she stayed some time, and had X-ray examinations, and I was so worried. But they didn't find anything wrong, so Mother came back home, and I was so happy. I'm afraid that desirable state did not last very long. That bad epidemic of Asian flu arrived and all of us caught it, Mother, me and Uncle. Unfortunately, Mother, who was sixty-six, never really recovered, gradually became worse, and early the next year the doctor said she must go back into hospital for more examinations. Before that could be arranged she took very poorly one day and an ambulance had to be sent for – luckily one of the nearby farms had a telephone. But all the local ambulances were busy and we had to wait for one to come from Richmond, which is many miles away. She died before the ambulance arrived at the hospital. I didn't go in the ambulance because there was the cattle work and all the arrangements to do, but a good neighbour, Mrs Britton, from High Birk Hatt, was with Mother.

A terrible blow it was. One of the worst things of my life. If Uncle hadn't been there to support me I do not know what would have become of me.

They brought Mother back to the chapel, which is disused these days. She didn't come back to Low Birk Hatt. But before the service the hearse drove to what we call the Hill's Gate – that's the gate from our land to the main road.

So in that way Mother bade farewell to Low Birk Hatt. It was Uncle's idea, and a very good one. What a dreadful day that was, and I was on my own because Uncle had to go away to attend to business matters. They don't stop even for funerals.

Mrs Britton very kindly put on a tea afterwards and

Mrs Fawcett, that grand person from the old days, was very comforting. But you could say that I have never really stopped missing Mother. She was such a heroine in her own way because it was not possible to give her the attention and comfort she deserved yet she never complained. I will never be the woman she was.

Uncle survived Mother by three years, and those were not easy times. He was older, seventy, and his legs began to give him such pain. I did my best, but it became more and more difficult to do the work on the farm and look after him. He had difficulty sleeping and sometimes would call out in the night for me to help him light his pipe. Towards the end he could no longer fend for himself and good neighbours used to come and help me get him up out of bed and into a chair. But then we had a spell of bad weather during hay-timing, a difficult situation at the best of times, and I simply could not manage. Uncle had been in bed for about a month by then, so the doctor arranged for him to go into hospital in Barnard Castle.

He never came back. Again through the help of kind neighbours I was able to visit him now and again, though not as often as one would have wished. One day the hospital rang Mrs Britton to say he had died, and to pass on the news to me. She even very kindly offered to attend to things, but I would not let her do that because I knew I had to face up to my responsibilities. So I went myself to see the undertaker, select the bearers, and arrange all the funeral details. It was a wintry day when Uncle was buried, with a bit of snow around. The service was held at the chapel and everyone went to the Kirk Inn at Romaldkirk afterwards. It wasn't the custom, really, but the landlord and his wife, Mr and Mrs Wallace, were friends of the Brittons and knew Uncle as well, so they agreed to lay on a nice tea.

There were no flowers. That wasn't a feature of funerals in Baldersdale and our family never had flowers, not even for Mother. We believed that flowers were for the living, and Uncle used often to quote some lines of poetry:

> *The flowers you are going to bring to my funeral,*
> *Bring them now, for I want to see them.*
> *The kind words you have to say about me,*
> *Say them now for I want to hear them.*

I decided to have a farm sale after Uncle went, and put up all the livestock for auction. There were about fifteen cattle, around a dozen sheep and a few lambs left over from the spring lambing. But I chose the wrong time when prices were depressed and there wasn't a great deal to come after all the expenses were paid. Apparently, if I had waited a bit longer prices would have been much higher. But then I was never much of a businesswoman and I had no close relatives left to turn to for help and advice.

I was all alone.

SEVEN

My Friends, the Beasts of the Field

L ife for Hannah Hauxwell then settled into a pattern which basically continues to this day. She kept one cow which each year produced one calf to send to market. The income from that sale, plus a little rent for pastures rented out to other farmers, produced a pitiful income which, when the first documentary presented Hannah to an amazed public in 1973, was running at about £5.50p a week.

Out of that she had to pay all expenses, including animal feed and coal, which left around five pounds a month for food. No running water, no electricity, and she couldn't even afford to keep a dog. After the transmission of the film, which conferred instant celebrity status, the economic situation improved dramatically, and she invested in more cattle to boost her income. But she had for several years been living a life which the word frugal does not even begin to describe accurately. And it was all compounded by a feeling not just of loneliness but more a sense of abandonment, as all the families she had known since childhood began to leave Baldersdale. And she was an only child.

It was to her animals that Hannah turned for companionship – even conversation! She lavished upon them the sort of affection she would have given to her family had there been any. They all had names. When Hannah made her first public bow, she was constantly in the company of an elderly white cow called Her Ladyship and her love for this awkward beast touched a certain public soft spot – the British are well known for their protective, caring attitude towards animals. The media are aware of this fact, and photographs of Hannah side by side with Her Ladyship featured in a hundred newspapers and more.

Well, Her Ladyship was rather special because she was with me for many years and supported me by producing calves for market. Not that I ever took them myself, because auction rings are a bit rough and noisy – places for men, really – so a kind neighbour would attend to things for me, such as arranging transport and attending the sale. I would just wait at home and hope for the best – you know, that a decent price would be bid. It was rather an important event for me in those days, as you can imagine. Just having one calf a year to sell instead of a sizeable number like most farmers.

Fourteen years we were together, Her Ladyship and me. I do not suppose most farmers would hang on that long. Inevitably she got down, and the day came when she had to go, for her own sake, really. Frank Bainbridge, the same man who took the calves to market, once again organized the necessary procedure. Another man came and he was canny, too – didn't make things worse. I didn't stay to see it happen, just went as far up the fields as I could go. I know these things are inevitable but . . .

These days I have Rosa, a daughter of Her Ladyship. She is fourteen and a half, and still in pretty good shape. There have been lots of others, of course, and I remember a lovely beast called Daisy who would have been grand. But nothing happened when I had her served so she had to go. Then there was The Bumpkin, and Septimus – I was particularly sorry to lose them. Nowadays I have three breeding cows, including Rosa, who is the senior beast. There's Patch, because she has a patch, and she has a daughter, Bunty. Then I have Puddles, sometimes called Bumble, because she is daft and somewhat nervous. I still have to carry water to her because sometimes she won't come out of the byre and follow her mother, which means that she is left all on her own. One feels sorry for the little ones in some circumstances and they nearly become like children –

but not quite. But I have to admit I become very attached to them and I know it's a fault.

When I was a child we had two bay-coloured horses, and I later got to know them very well. Dick and Snip they were called, and Daddy was quite attached to Dick. He was only small, but a very willing little man even though he suffered an accident when he was young. I recall the time when Daddy had been very ill with pernicious anaemia and had to stay indoors for quite a while. Well, the first time he came out of the door when he was a little better, he shouted for Dick, who was in the top pasture. And Dick came galloping down to greet him – it was quite something. I used to ride both horses in the early days to take them to be shod over to Lowson's Smithy at Romaldkirk. Later on we took them to Woody Swinbank's at Mickleton, but that's been turned into a pub now, appropriately called the Blacksmith's Arms.

When I got a bit older I worked with the horses in the fields, particularly at haytiming. Snip, the mare, wasn't as friendly or cooperative as Dick, and used to be very awkward when I was sweeping the hay with her. Once, the sweeping machinery fell over and I sprained my wrist.

Uncle brought his own horse when he took over at Low Birk Hatt, an old grey mare called Madge. She had a foal one year, and Uncle thought a lot of her.

One night he was over the moors around North Stainmore and had to return home at dead of night. There wasn't a light anywhere, but Uncle just gave Madge her head and she brought him safely home. But she got too old eventually and so did Dick and Snip, so we had to send them away.

Then we bought a lovely horse called Prince with much better breeding than the others. He possessed a lovely long tail which swept right down to the ground and it was a lovely sight to see him turn round. Uncle was always wanting to have that tail cut shorter and we had quite a few battles about it, but I won and Prince kept his long tail. Because of his fine pedigree he was a little bit more highly strung than the others and would set off rather sharply. He had no really bad faults but you had to be careful that nothing startled him, such as a bird suddenly rising, and on one occasion he did bolt. Once, I had a rather nerve-racking experience with him when I was working the horse rake in the lower field.

I got into a mess with the reins when I was turning and Prince began to reverse towards the edge of the ghyll by the side of the field, which had a sharp drop. I couldn't stop him and I was so frightened that horse, machine and me were going over that I jumped off. But I kept hold of the reins and Prince just stopped in time. I still dream about Prince.

In later years we borrowed Blossom, a big Clydesdale-type mare, from John Sayer at West New Houses, and eventually we bought her. But she had a strange temperament and we were told by one man who worked for John Sayer and had helped to break her in that she wasn't right in the head. She had a foal with us during the dreadful winter of 1947, and her behaviour became even worse, so much so that our good neighbour Mr Britton said she wasn't fit for a young woman like me to work with and insisted I borrow his horse Bobby, a very even-tempered animal.

The last horse we ever had was the best, a plump little Dales pony called Thomas. He didn't just eat to live, that horse, he lived to eat, which was obvious when you saw how fat he was. But he was the most pleasant animal to work with. Some horses become excited and upset if something goes a bit wrong when they are in harness, such as chains or ropes becoming entangled around their feet. They will often rear or kick out and generally create a real commotion. But Thomas never bothered, just let you get on quietly with sorting out any mess like that. As long as you fed him plenty, he would be most cooperative.

Over the years I have done all kinds of work with horses, haymaking, spreading and harrowing manure and hauling coal down from the road on a sledge. Haymaking meant long days and tough work, all by hand.

At one time we would have to hire a man in for a month, eating with us but sleeping in the barn. Everything depended on the weather and if your luck was out the hired man's time could be up and not much hay in. I still remember the names of some of the men we hired over the years – there was Billy Lockie, Mark Dent, and an Irishman called John Boyne.

Childhood memories are always best, of course, and everything was so much better when my father was alive. In those days we would always start the haymaking at Hury, a parcel of land we owned two miles down the road. It had a house which once had a thatched roof, but it had gone derelict and a tree had started growing in the middle of it. Just the three of us, my parents and me, would go down to Hury and stay there for two or three weeks, or until the work was done. We left the older ones in the family to look after Low Birk Hatt, do the milking and other chores, and we went down with the horses. We must have made quite a sight trailing along the road with scythes, rakes, forks, the sledge and the sweep, mowing machine, and our food in a basket. And a bed! The house still had a good warm loft, so we all used to sleep there. Oh, I did love our times together at Hury, with Mother cooking supper over the fire in an old iron grate and the nights so romantic and balmy. There were lots of wild roses and foxgloves growing around the lanes and fields and you could smell the hawthorn and rowan tree blossom. Those summer nights at Hury will stay with me for ever. Everything comes to life in the summer with the long days, the moon to illuminate the darkness, and the birds calling to each other in the trees. My parents used to sit and talk about going to live there permanently one day! I know they loved the place and Daddy planned to mend and restore it for us. But that dream went when he died.

Apart from haymaking, the other important events in Baldersdale, or any other farming dale, centred around the animals, and we kept the usual selection. After the cattle, the sheep were economically the most important, followed by the pigs, hens and geese.

Lambing time could be quite hectic since we had about sixty sheep at one time, and a good crop of healthy lambs to be sent to market was essential. We also had to shear and dip them every year and friends would come to help. The Fawcetts had a sheep dip and we would take ours there, but the shearing was quite a problem for me. Uncle used to tie the legs of the poor beast and then I could get a fleece off, but it was a method expert shearers used to scorn. Trouble was, I just couldn't hold the sheep properly – but then I have to admit I never liked doing it. It wasn't the sheep, it was that greasy wool that caused the trouble. I liked the sheep well enough, particularly when they were lambs.

Sometimes when the little ones were weakly or had been abandoned by their mothers, we would have to take them inside and feed them by hand.

Our wool used to go to a firm called Ackroyds down in the textile area of the West Riding of Yorkshire, but years before the war a gentleman called Watson Taylor would visit the dale. He was a representative of a mill called Waddells and he had a strange-looking horse-drawn vehicle, square shaped with high sides. He used to take some wool, but mainly he was there to sell and his cart carried samples. He had some lovely tartan coloured rugs which I used to go and admire over at Clove Lodge, where he would take lodgings for the night. People would give him fleeces to take away to be finished off, perhaps coloured, at his mill. I know Mother traded with him from time to time, and once sent a quantity of wool away to another mill and had some back as grey blankets. But they weren't the same superior quality as those Mr Watson Taylor brought because they wore out. The tartan rugs from Waddells would still be going today, I imagine. I haven't seen the like in many years.

Both Grandma and Mother were clever with their hands, making mats and quilts. Grandma laboured for years with her frames and turned out all the mats for the house. I have still got two quilts that she made, which have been in use for as long as I can recall.

Mother knitted a white cotton quilt before she married, which I treasure to this day. I have done a bit myself, but possess neither the ability nor the patience to do fine work. I prefer thick wool which gets done rather more quickly, and during the war I unravelled some of Grandma's things and knitted them up again. In those days we had to use an oil wool, which was all right after you washed it, if somewhat coarse. I knitted myself a dress from that which started off fawn, but we ran out of that colour and I had to finish it off in blue. Maybe it wasn't the last word in smartness – far from it – but it was very warm and comfortable, if rather too big. I made a scarf and then set off to knit socks, but got into a mess with the difficult parts and Mother finished them off. The last thing I knitted was a red pullover for Uncle which I have yet. But I was never as good as Grandma who produced lovely crochet work with intricate floral designs. My work tends to be more durable than artistic.

Of course, it was nice to know that some of our things were made from the wool from our own sheep. I had my favourites, of course, particularly one which I called Nanny Bateson. It came to me as a gift, a little black-faced lamb sent to me by the Batesons who were farming Briscoe at the time. She grew up into a grand ewe and produced a lot of lambs for us. I had other pet lambs, but Nanny Bateson was the first and the best-remembered.

We sent the lambs to be sold at auction in the autumn. A little man called Maurice Tarn was the auctioneer, and the sale was held in the fields alongside the Strathmore Arms. Other income came from the calves we had to spare and everyone would lose quite a bit of sleep when the cows were calving since the event would invariably happen in the middle of the night and it was often necessary to play midwife in case of complications. Losing a lamb or two was not unusual, but a dead calf was a serious matter.

I didn't care much for the hens and geese but I had quite a high opinion of the pigs. Most people think that pigs are dirty and ignorant, but I had many happy times with them. They let me look after and feed two piglets when I was a little girl and they were really friendly and affectionate. I used to play with them for hours on end and they tore a big hole in the back of my coat during one rough and tumble. I didn't give them names, which was just as well because they both had to go to be killed.

Later on a neighbour sold us a reckling – that's the runt of the litter, too small to be really valuable – and I did name him. Joss grew up into a very pleasant pig, and some can be very temperamental and even nasty, and he stayed with us whilst Mother was alive. Then I'm sorry to say he made a bacon pig.

I have known some pigs which were really rather clean. It helps if you keep the place tidy and regularly mucked out, and we did have one which kept its bed and its toilet place quite separate. Oddly enough our pigs didn't do so well at market. To us they were lovely looking animals, but, would you credit it, they said they were too fat!

Pig killing was quite an event in the dale and had to take place when there was an 'R' in the month because it was wise to avoid the warmer months since refrigerators were unknown in the dale. And because one would share with neighbours, it was rather spaced out so that people could benefit over a longer period.

I used to avoid being present at the killings. When I was a child they killed one close by me and I heard the squealing. So always after that I would make sure I had a job to do as far away as possible from the scene, because it upset me a lot. I made my escape, you would say, and I know it was the coward's way out, because I have to confess that I thoroughly enjoyed the proceeds.

For some years a man used to come in and do the deed, but Uncle got on with it himself later round by the stable, using a humane killer. Then the throat would be cut to drain off the blood to make into black puddings – I wasn't too good with the blood either, but it was tasty afterwards.

The pig would be hung up on a big strong hook and there was much to-ing and fro-ing with kettles of boiling water to help scrape off the bristles and extract the entrails. Nothing was wasted. The liver was usually eaten first and some of the tasty bits, like the spare ribs, sausages and chines – that's pieces of the backbone – would be sent round to friends and neighbours.

The kitchen then became a hive of industry, with the fat being cut up and rendered for lard, kept in a big earthenware pot. Brawn would be made from the trotters and the ears, and then there was the head. I never had a lot to do with the pig's head, but it did make lovely potted meat. It all took a lot of hot water and big pans.

The flitches – that's the hams – were laid down in salt and saltpetre to cure, then hung up on hooks. Mother used to put a bit of sugar on as well. I cannot understand why our pigs were criticized for being too fat because the meat was so sweet and tender, almost like chicken.

I always helped with the sausages. Uncle used to do a bit because he liked fiddling with machines, and the one we had in the early days was borrowed and not really suitable. It was a big machine which I think had not been set up right – it seemed to have more blades than necessary. But Uncle liked to play around with it. Mother and I were much happier when we acquired our own machine and we could get on with it together. Those sausages were a credit to Mother because she knew just the seasoning they required, and we would hang them up in the kitchen for people to eat as they pleased. One would stand on a chair and cut a piece off at mealtimes. I preferred them when they were fresh because they had a bit of a tang later on, but they were so good that the thought of them makes me hungry.

EIGHT

Housekeeping . . . and Health

Public exposure on television and the continual attention of the rest of the media did have a marked effect on Hannah Hauxwell. She insists that it was entirely benign. And, remarkably, it changed her personality not one whit. She preserved her dignity, independence and way of life. What it did do was confer material benefits, which were desperately needed at Low Birk Hatt. The threat of malnutrition receded and vanished for ever, and the twentieth century finally arrived with a team from the North Eastern Electricity Board. However, there are still serious problems.

It all started when a man called Frank Somers wrote to me and enclosed a photograph of himself and his wife Pauline and their little girl called Hayley. A very nice letter it was too, but just one of many from people who had seen me on television. Indeed it was difficult to cope with all the letters in the early days after the first programme.

Then he turned up and explained his ideas about bringing electricity to Low Birk Hatt. It seemed to be an impossible dream at first because of the distance and the difficulties. And, of course, the cost – that ran into thousands. But he was so moved by the film that he launched a campaign to raise the money at the place where he worked. That was called Lancro Chemicals, a rather large firm in Eccles, near Manchester. He managed to borrow a copy of the film and showed it in the works canteen and raised most of the money. Yorkshire Television made good the shortfall and the Electricity Board set to work. Those poor men had a lot of problems driving in the poles to carry the lines and were obliged to use explosives on the last stretch over my land because they came across solid rock. Then Frank arrived one weekend with a team of his work-mates to wire the place up and install the plugs and light fittings. We had a grand switch-on with cameras from Yorkshire Television recording the moment for their regional magazine programme, *Calendar*, and all the newspapers covered it, too. A lady from Doncaster wrote and offered me a cooker, so Frank and his friends went to pick it up, overhaul it and bring it here. That, and the electric kettle, given to me by a good friend, are a great blessing.

Someone also presented me with an electric washer but I have never been able to use it because there isn't water in the house and I wouldn't be able to understand it anyway. But after the second programme Yorkshire Television installed block heaters throughout the house in lieu of a fee, so Low Birk Hatt was heated properly for the very first time. It was just as well because the back boiler in the kitchen split in two about fifteen years ago and I haven't been able to light a fire in the grate since.

Until then I had done my cooking, such as it was, on that fire. Things were not very good in those days, and the financial situation was very worrying. There was no great amount of money coming in and one was continually minding the pennies. The food bill had risen to five pounds a month and, with being so tired with all the work, I suppose I neglected myself. I lost some weight and felt ill enough to go to the doctor who sent me to hospital in Northallerton. Altogether I was away from Low Birk Hatt for two months and those kind neighbours of mine came to the rescue once again and looked after the animals.

I must say that I enjoyed my time in hospital. I made a lot of friends and was introduced to the wonders of television for the first time.

Nowadays I am a lot better placed and able to eat better because of the electric cooker. I tend to have a lot of sausage and bacon because it's easier and my time is somewhat at a premium with around a dozen cattle to care for. But occasionally I will take the big pan and fill it with onions, carrots and potatoes for a grand stew. Washing up is a problem because of the business of having to fetch water and heat it up, so I do not bother much with tinned soup, which can make pans such a mess. And I don't stand the cans in hot water in case it marks the bottom of the pan and spoils it.

As you might imagine my monthly food bill has gone up quite appreciably, far more than the five pounds a month just before the programme *Too Long a Winter* was made. When you count in a bag of calf cake and the general groceries, including the eggs, it will come to more than thirty pounds these days.

That will include the meat for the dog and brown bread for the cat. I prefer white bread myself, because it makes better toast, but I always get a brown sliced for the cat, which likes a little bit of butter with it.

Being able to afford a dog now is another advantage. I have had one or two in recent years, mostly given to me by kind people, but things didn't work out with them. But now I have Timmy, a nice little man and a grand companion. When I fall asleep in my chair he always sits on my lap. He's a Jack Russell so I'm hoping he might do something about the rodent problem at Low Birk Hatt. All farms have rats and mice but in recent years they have been coming through from the barn into the house and getting into the furniture. I'm afraid I have to suspend my perishables, like bread, cheese, butter and vegetables, from the ceiling in plastic bags or they would get at them.

I know the rats are a worry because they are so dangerous and can contaminate food. Last winter I came face to face with one on the landing – I don't know which of us was the more scared. After that I made a habit of sending Timmy upstairs ahead of me when it's time to go to bed.

Now I am very well aware that a number of good friends worry a lot about my situation and my health, particularly in the winter, but I manage quite nicely, thank you. I know people imagined I was much older than I was when they saw the first film because some newspapers referred to me as 'the Old Lady of the Dales'. But I was forty-six at the time! Now I am a pensioner, rising sixty-three, and some people say I have changed very little. Of course, I do have a few problems, but I have good caring doctors who have prescribed medication.

For the last two years I have had to take two tablets a day. It's for what the doctor calls angina. Such a nuisance it is because it's a condition which makes you tire more easily, leaving you short of energy and breath. It can be very annoying when you are wanting to hurry, chasing the cattle up a hill or something. I also have some other tablets, smaller ones, which I have to take if I get a pain across the chest and it persists . . . what I call a chuntering thing. There can be this dreadful tired feeling with it, too, which is very frustrating when you know time's getting on and you know you cannot delay the work any longer. I will take two in that sort of situation. Otherwise I seldom touch them. I think it better for you if you can avoid things like that, although I have no authority for saying so. I do understand that some people with my condition have to take goodness knows how many tablets of one sort or another each and every day, so I suppose I am fortunate.

My eyes are another problem. I was a little foolish in earlier years before the electric light, trying to read and sew by the light of an oil lamp and pressing on when I should have stopped and rested my eyes. It must be ten years since I went to the optician and I keep promising myself I will go when the opportunity presents itself, because I love to read. In the days when I had more time to spare I would read any book I could lay my hands on and particularly enjoyed anything about foreign lands.

I am often asked what if I had an accident or I collapsed and there was no one around to help. But there is an arrangement to cater for an emergency of that kind. The two local policemen came around one day and suggested I place a red light in a window which could be seen by as many neighbours or passers-by as possible. I was to switch it on if in serious trouble. Richard Megson, who runs the hostel over at Blackton, very kindly came over to fix it up for me. I do hope and pray that I will never have the need to use it.

NINE

Travel . . . from Tommy's Bus to the Savoy and Buckingham Palace

Until she was approaching her half-century Hannah was probably the least travelled person any-where in the northern counties. Yet, paradoxically, in another way she has more experience than most. On several occasions visitors to Low Birk Hatt, in the middle of discussing their planned holiday or business trips abroad, were startled by Hannah's detailed know-ledge of the places they were due to visit. Especially if they happened to be Paris, Venice or Florence. Hannah read extensively about the classic cities when her eyes permitted such luxuries and still absorbs information from radio and television like a sponge. She has a fine appreciation of art, literature, music and architecture, and clearly a thirst for travel.

I have often thought how interesting and useful it would be to have a globe in the house. Then one could spin it round when news, travel or holiday programmes on radio and television specify certain places and you could see where they were in relation to Britain and the rest of the world. Marvellous as a map is, a globe gives you a far clearer idea of the overall situation, with the world being round.

Mind you, travel was very much an academic thing for me until the television programme and even now I can scarcely say I am a travelled person. These days everyone seems to be hopping on and off jets if only to go to the Spanish holiday resorts, but I have never left these shores. Indeed, the furthest I had ever been in my pre-television life was a day trip to Loch Lomond on a bus. Before the war, a man called Tommy Oliver ran a bus service for the people of Baldersdale. Now there was a pleasant, outgoing and jolly man, and I am glad to say he had a long and happy life. Tommy's bus was the very first form of public transport that I encountered because he came every Wednesday to the head of the dale to take us to Barnard Castle.

The bus held about twenty people, but it carried all manner of other things. I have seen poultry and rabbits and large baskets of butter and eggs sharing seats down to Barnard Castle. I think the fare in later years was half a crown return, and he would park up near the post office, so that people could come and leave their shopping with him instead of humping it about the streets. The return journey was supposed to start at half past three but there would always be a few people missing. But Tommy was so good-natured about everything and he would sally forth and start asking people where his strays might be. Sometimes the bus didn't set off until nearly four o'clock. One day Tommy had to let someone else drive and that man set off at three-thirty prompt. That caused some consternation and I don't think the same person deputized again.

Tommy did all the pre-war Chapel outings. I had my first glimpse of the sea on a Sunday School outing to Redcar when I was about ten. I couldn't swim, never have been able to, and I didn't go out on a boat because along with the rest of the family I have always been afraid of water. The sole exception was Mother – she liked riding in a boat and went out with her close friend Mrs Fawcett, who took her boys along, too.

The last trip on Tommy's bus was to the Lake District. Then he and his wife retired to take on the post office at Romaldkirk, some time before the outbreak of war. He delivered the letters and ran a little bit of a farm he owned, whilst his wife looked after the post office. The Oliver family was long established in Romaldkirk and they had a shop selling meal and other products. Tommy was one of a number of boys, and he also had one sister.

After the war a man called Alec Howson in Barnard Castle ran the trips and it was with him that we went to Loch Lomond. Now that was a feat of ability, patience and sheer physical endurance. We left Clove Lodge at six o'clock in the morning and arrived back at four o'clock the following morning. Alec drove all the way, with breaks, of course, and it was a marvellous experience.

We went with Alec for quite a few years, and sometimes Mother would come too. She was with me on one occasion when we went to Saltburn, where they had some Italian gardens which I liked very much. It was there that I first heard 'The Skater's Waltz'. I couldn't work out whether it was a band playing it or a record but that tune will always be associated with the trip to Saltburn.

Of course, we have our own local beauty spot, High Force, which is a spectacular waterfall further up Teesdale. I have only ever been there once with a family related to me; I suppose they are my second cousins, Norman and Lizzie Bayles, who farmed at Stoop Hill, a small place just outside of Mickleton. Norman Bayles was a cousin to my father and was related to Mother through the Tallentire family. Although the family ties were not very close, we have always been very friendly and spent quite a lot of time together. It was usual for us to call when we took the horses over to Mickleton to be shod. Mother and Uncle would come as well and we had some lovely times together, full of music and laughter. Music was very important to Norman and occasionally he would come over and invite me to concerts and films. Once, Reginald Forte, the famous organist, came to Middleton in Teesdale and I had the pleasure of attending that concert. Norman and Lizzie had two daughters. Marjorie, the youngest, was a schoolgirl in those days. Lizzie used to lend me books which I looked forward to getting. We would go to Middleton Carnival with them when time and circumstances permitted, and one lovely June day we went to High Force and had a picnic. We sat on a tree that had been felled and ate some very tasty ham sandwiches – one of the few picnics I have ever been to. Of course, my horizons broadened considerably after the documentary. First of all I was invited to lunch in Leeds and they sent the helicopter for me, piloted by Captain John Leeson, who had done all the flying for the aerial shots in the film. I had been his guest in the air very briefly before when I was taken up to see Low Birk Hatt as a bird would see it, and I found it a thrilling experience, quite the best way to travel. Leeds was the first city I had ever visited and when I was taken by car to the television studios I had my first encounter with revolving doors, which I found rather strange. I'm not very good with things like that. I met some very interesting people, including Fred Trueman. Now, I knew he was connected with sport but I didn't know whether it was cricket or football. So I had to ask him to make sure, and he was very nice about it. I really enjoyed our conversation.

I went back home by taxi because it was too dark for the helicopter to fly, and I'm afraid I do not travel as well by road. But some tablets were kindly provided and they did alleviate the problem. However, I had a funny reaction when the taxi arrived back in Baldersdale – my legs went and I could hardly walk. But the Atkinsons at Clove Lodge looked after me, gave me a cup of tea and saw me safely home.

From the travel point of view things carried on a bit from there in a local sense. I was invited to open functions in various parts of the Yorkshire Dales and quite a surprising number of people turned up. I had also had a very enjoyable weekend in Sheffield when the Salvation Army invited me to make an appearance. People would send cars up that rough track to Low Birk Hatt to make sure I travelled in style. I made a lot of new friends, some of whom are still in touch.

I was also astounded at the amount of mail that arrived – too much, really, because I just could not deal properly with it all and I was worried in case people thought me impolite. But one day in 1977 a rather special envelope arrived, bearing an engraved card inviting me to be a guest of honour at the Women of the Year lunch at the Savoy Hotel in London. Now, I know it was a great honour but I could see no way of accepting, so I put it on the mantelpiece and more or less prepared to forget all about it. However, one of my many visitors saw it and told Barry Cockcroft, the gentleman who produced and directed my film for Yorkshire Television. Next thing I knew he was at the door, insisting that I accept the invitation and asking me if I was prepared to make another documentary with him! He was preparing a series of six documentaries with the overall title of *Once in a Lifetime* and said the situation regarding the Women of the Year lunch fitted in perfectly.

He offered to make all the arrangements, such as organize the travel and someone to look after the cattle for me, so I agreed. After all I had never been to London and it is one's capital city! Barry called the film *Hannah Goes to Town.*

Well, it was all a big thrill. We filmed on the train to London and I was told at one stage that we were proceeding at one hundred miles an hour. It did not seem possible.

When we arrived at King's Cross I was told for the sake of reality I must find my own way to the Savoy Hotel, although the film crew would be close by in case of emergency. They filmed everything, of course. I had a bit of trouble on the Underground with all those automatic machines but one of the station staff spotted that I was in difficulty and came to my aid. I negotiated my way to Piccadilly – those illuminations are a splendid sight – and after a few more adventures finally arrived at the Savoy.

Well, the place was just a dream . . . completely out of this world. I was escorted to the fifth floor and shown in to a riverside suite which was named after Sir Charles Chaplin, because he always used to stay there when he visited London. I had an enormous bedroom, and a separate sitting room and bathroom. The wardrobe was unbelievable, you could walk in at one door and out of the other, several yards away. I was told that Sir Noël Coward also stayed in the same suite quite regularly.

There was a very long and comfortable settee in front of the window which had a view of the River Thames which mesmerized me to such an extent that I could scarcely tear myself away to go to bed. There were so many lights, and all sorts of colours, too. I saw ships and all manner of boats, and I was surprised by all the greenery just below the window. I thought how nice it would be to just stroll across the road and look at the river, and it appears to be quite simple until you get there and meet I don't know how many lanes of traffic.

If anyone ever gets the opportunity to stay at the Savoy, then my advice is – take it! Apart from the temperature in my suite being a little too high for someone used to Low Birk Hatt, the entire experience was truly a once-in-a-lifetime thing. When it was time to leave and I was waiting for the car to take me back to the station for the journey back, I have to confess that I shed a tear or two.

But there were so many wonderful moments in between. We had dinner and a floor show, when part of the floor rose up as if by magic and a cabaret was presented. The next day was the big event and I wore a nice new dress in blue and fawn which I bought from Shepherd's in Barnard Castle.

Well, it was absolute chaos when I went down to the Press reception before the Women of the Year lunch. They swamped me with their cameras, tape recorders and notebooks. Not that I'm complaining because I realized they had a job to do, but they were all firing their questions at once, and I do like to give a civil, considered reply. Anyway, I did some radio interviews and I was quite taken aback when I found myself over the front page of the *Evening Standard*. I cannot imagine what they were all thinking about.

Afterwards, Lady Mary Wilson, Sir Harold's wife, came and had a chat. She said she had seen the pro-gramme and wondered if it had spoiled anything for me, but I was able to reassure her that it had improved my life. She seemed very reassured. Then I was asked to join the small group selected to meet the Royal personage in attendance, the Duchess of Gloucester. We had quite a conversation. I said that I understood she came from the Continent, and she told me that she was born in Denmark. I asked if she liked living in this country. She was so nice, and later wrote me a letter in her own hand, which is a treasured possession.

Later I had the honour and privilege of meeting Odette Churchill, the heroine of the French Resistance, someone I had admired for years, ever since reading about her exploits when she received her medal after the war. She had seen the film, too, and I received a letter some time later from her husband, Mr Hallows, telling me that Odette was not in the best of health and they were moving house. So I met three very special ladies that day, and talked to a number of other nice people.

The lunch itself was held in a huge room and there was a constant babble of noise. I am not quite sure who it was I sat next to because I am such a slow eater that I did not have much time for conversation. I am not able to eat and talk at the same time, so I apologized to my neighbours for this.

The Duchess of Gloucester and the sailing lady, Clare Francis, were among the speakers, and there was an interruption when some people staged a demonstration. I thought it was in support of the IRA but it could have been some other organization, such as the Women's

Liberation people. Anyway it didn't spoil anything, and the whole event will be a vivid memory for ever.

Before leaving London I saw the sights, from the Tower to Trafalgar Square, and I also had a wander through Soho which I remember not so much for its more dubious side but for all the stalls of fruit and vegetables, every type, colour and description. I went into Fortnum and Mason and then across the road to speak to a gentleman dressed in very fine livery and top hat who stood at the entrance to Burlington Arcade. I also saw the statue of Sir Winston Churchill outside the Houses of Parliament and the monument to Edith Cavell; I have a book about her life.

One or two people in the streets talked to me, including the man who sold the corn to feed the pigeons in Trafalgar Square – in fact, he even gave me a kiss. But my other impression of London was that it could be a very lonely place if you were there on your own without friends or relations. Everybody seemed to be rushing around looking straight ahead. People don't seem to look at other people, whereas in the towns and villages in the north that I have known the locals will bid you good day or smile as you go in and out of shops or even just crossing the street.

I really think, although I would not be prepared to put it to the test, that you could go out in the streets of London in your nightdress and nobody would notice. Of course, that might suit me because I could wear my old rags and not attract attention. I rather pity the young who live in London because they must be having a particularly difficult time.

Of course, I was insulated from the more unpleasant aspects of city life, wallowing in the luxury of the Savoy, being waited on hand and foot. All that beautiful silver and the linen, which was fresh every time, and the staff were so friendly. I had a most interesting conversation about Italian opera with a waiter called Giovanni, who was as enthusiastic as me about Verdi.

Naturally, I went to see Buckingham Palace, not dreaming on that occasion that I would not only see it again but actually enter the premises. I was invited a year or so later to the Royal Garden Party held in honour of the Queen Mother's eightieth birthday, so there I was off again to London with a film crew in attendance. I bought another dress in Barnard Castle made from very fine material with a flared skirt, and the *Daily Mail* kindly presented me with a broad-brimmed floral hat and a pair of white gloves to take some very nice photographs. That hat has been to Buckingham Palace twice because I lent it to a friend who was invited to a later garden party.

When I arrived at the Palace gates with my invitation card I was somewhat taken aback when two or three in the crowd around the railings recognized me and asked for autographs – in that place of all places! I did not know what to do or where to go, so I approached a very nice policeman, told him I was from the country and asked which gate I should use. He explained everything to me and I went across a big courtyard, through a door into a large hall, then up some stairs and along a landing turning left towards an outside terrace down to the lawns at the rear of the Palace.

Although it was July, the weather was rather cold and blustery and some people had wisely brought their raincoats, but not me! I was advised by a friend that it wouldn't be quite the thing to go in raincoat and wellies! Hundreds of people were there and I only saw the Queen at the beginning when she came out with Prince Philip and the Queen Mother and stood at the head of the terrace whilst a band played the National Anthem.

Some gentlemen dressed in grey whom I took to be equerries had organized us so that the Royal party had two corridors, flanked by people, to walk down. I'm afraid they came down the steps and chose the path leading away from me, so I only saw those three at a distance. Several people were presented and it would have been nice to have been closer. Not that I had any wish to be presented – I mean, there is all this protocol and etiquette to be observed and I may have blundered.

I was there on my own, because the Yorkshire Television film crew had been positioned on the roof of
the Palace, and would have been quite at a loss but
a lady from the *Yorkshire Post* spotted me and kindly
accompanied me for a little while. She pointed out
different people, including Prince Andrew, who was
standing quite close by talking to a group of people. I
wouldn't have known who it was but for her courtesy.
She also fetched me tea and refreshment from one of the
marquees. I enjoyed bread and butter, little flat pan-
cakes and a nice light fruit cake. I avoided the chocolate
cake because I thought it looked a little sickly.

Then I plucked up the courage to start moving
around on my own and began walking down a path
when the gentleman in grey asked people to stand
aside, and I stepped well back. Along came Prince
Charles and Princess Anne. My main impression was
that they both had very fair hair and small features,
which surprised me because their photographs in the
newspapers give a different impression, particularly in
the case of Prince Charles. Up to then I thought he
had dark hair. Princess Anne smiled at me as she went
by, or perhaps it was just my imagination. I wish I had
summoned up the nerve to smile back.

After it was all over there was another strange and
thrilling event when a car whisked me to the *News at
Ten* studios where I was interviewed by someone in

Leeds. It was most peculiar sitting there among all the cameras, wearing an earphone and talking to someone more than two hundred miles away.

That wonderful day ended on a most romantic note when I was taken to a lovely dinner in a large hotel, still wearing my floral dress. A very gallant gentleman at the next table came over, and for no particular reason, kissed my hand!

TEN

The True Daughter of Balder . . .
from Another Point of View

Since it was undisputedly colonized by the Vikings, it is reasonable to assume that Baldersdale experienced a long and vivid history. So it is hardly surprising that the place has bred a line of hardy, taciturn beings who, accustomed from birth to fighting the elements simply to survive, are not given to public demonstrations of any kind of emotion. It would probably take an earthquake or an overnight plunge in the market value of Swaledale sheep (or both) to raise the communal eyebrow. Indeed, in the last two decades there has been only one event of sufficient gravity to create stunned, almost disbelieving debate among past and present Baldersdale folk – Hannah Hauxwell herself.

One day she was poor little Hannah from up Birk Hatt, struggling on her own since her folk died, the shy, quiet lass destined for a life of continued obscurity. The next, she was Hannah Hauxwell, international celebrity. Suddenly, their sleepy dale was full of people carrying parcels and speaking many strange

tongues, all clamouring to be advised of the where-
abouts of Hannah Hauxwell. The general astonish-
ment lingers to this day.

It could have led to a certain amount of resentment,
particularly when the material benefits flowed in for
Hannah. Fortunately, it is in the nature of these people
to be supportive, particularly towards their own. And
Hannah, whatever happens, will always be one of
their own. When Baldersdalians talk about her these
days it is with an undiminished affection. There is a
shared pride for the fame and attention she has
brought to the dale. It is illuminating to listen to their
own experiences of life in this isolated corner and
their memories of Hannah and the rest of the Hauxwells, since it adds depth and substance to the seasons
of Hannah's own life.

The Norsemen who battled their way into the northern uplands (one of their leaders rejoiced in the name
of Erik Bloodaxe) must have been almost as poetic as
they were bloodthirsty. They gave such lyrical names
to almost every place they seized, thus perpetuat-
ing their memory for ever. When they marched into
Hannah's birthplace they elected to commemorate
their god Balder, which has some curious significance
for Hannah's life.

Balder was a son of the most senior god, Odin, and

one version of the legend says he was blessed with the gift of immunity from harm. However, it was not total since, oddly, mistletoe would be the death of him. As long as he could avoid this seasonal parasite, he would live for ever. But it got him in the end. The blind god, Hod, enraged by the false words of the evil Loki, hurled a bunch of the stuff at him and Balder fell lifeless to the ground. Even then he could have been saved, so the story goes, if the giantess Thokk had agreed to shed life-giving tears for him, but for unspecified reasons she refused.

There is general agreement that Balder was not exactly a dynamic deity – indeed, he has been described as 'a passive, suffering figure'. When you consider the life of Hannah Hauxwell, and the privations she has quietly suffered for most of her life, it is reasonable to describe her as a true daughter of Balder.

'Sweet . . . shy . . . sad' . . . the same words are echoed when you speak of Hannah to those who lived and farmed alongside her over the years. One went so far as to describe her life as 'tragic'. They all, without exception, point to the harsh circumstances of the Hauxwells, which would have crushed less resilient souls. Whereas all the other farmsteads had either lusty young sons to work the land and tend the animals to improve their living standards, or were able to afford to hire in permanent labour, the Hauxwells were supporting four elderly relatives at one stage, had no sons (Hannah was an only child) and were finally dealt a cruel blow when Hannah's father became mortally ill.

Their immediate neighbours helped the Hauxwells with a willingness which speaks volumes for the selfless, caring attitude common among Dalesfolk. Crisis invariably brings out the best in rural people and Baldersdale, when the occasion demanded, could act like one large family. Time and again, sons or hired hands were sent vaulting over the dry-stone walls to Low Birk Hatt when it became obvious that the Hauxwells were on the point of dropping with exhaustion as they struggled to finish their haymaking or sheep shearing. Hannah herself is quick to acknowledge this magnanimity.

William Bayles Hauxwell fought mightily to keep pace with the ceaseless tide of farmwork at a time when mechanization and all the labour-saving devices now taken for granted in agriculture were but a distant dream in Baldersdale. The memory of his unremitting burden and the courageous way he tackled it is still fresh in the minds of his old neighbours and friends.

John Thwaites, one of the sons at High Birk Hatt,

just up the pasture from the Hauxwells, now in his early seventies and living a happy retirement with his wife, Marie, in a cottage near Lartington, a short distance from Baldersdale, vividly recalls the painful life of William as he tilled the eighty sparse acres of his farm.

'Aye, but he were a nice fellow. And what a worker . . . he worked every hour that God sent to try and keep on top of that place. He was very like Hannah in his attitude and manner – very genteel – and I've noticed that as she grows older she looks more and more like him. Most other people say she resembles her mother, so maybe she's a good mix. Now Hannah's mother was a lady . . . a real, proper lady was Lydia. Everyone agreed on that.

'But what a tragic family they were. Every other farm in the dale was blessed with children able to share the work but all they had was elderly folk who did their level best to help but were just too old and infirm. The sad thing is that William's anaemia could have been mended now. But then there was nothing they could do for him. He took cold, developed pneumonia and that was the end of him.

'I was only young at the time, but I can still recall the funeral, and the flat cart with his coffin being pulled up the field by his horse. My mother helped to cater for the funeral tea, which were community affairs with everyone helping.

'There were a few deaths in the dale which wouldn't have happened in later years. My own brother, Leonard, died from Bright's disease – that's a kidney complaint but I think they call it by a different name these days. Nowadays they have those machines to keep people alive and well.'

Trained medical assistance was hard to come by in Baldersdale during the childhood of Hannah. John Thwaites describes how the Dalesfolk, as in most other situations, organized themselves to cope with the deficiency. There were unpaid, unqualified 'nurses', usually senior ladies of the dale who possessed all the medical folklore and herbal remedies handed down from generation to generation. They were prepared to sit by the bedsides of sick neighbours to relieve the burden of their families and allow them to save their energy to cope with the farmwork. There were also recognized 'midwives' who would attend confine-ments and run matters efficiently until the doctor arrived – and quite often when he didn't (or couldn't, because of distance or foul weather).

There is no doubt that in times of trouble Balders-dale was a very united place – but there were, never-theless, some curious divisions. Full membership of the 'family' was not automatic just because you lived there. John Thwaites, born in the dale in 1917, was very much aware of certain subtleties.

'My family were interlopers, and we always knew it. It didn't matter that I was born in Baldersdale, my father wasn't. He was a Swaledale man who arrived in 1910 and that made all the difference. I was never considered a true Baldersdale man.

'My father used to tell a story that shows what I mean. One day, soon after he arrived in the dale, he had reason to go to another farm and overheard a conversation between two old ladies. They were lamenting that it was a sad day because outsiders were coming into the dale and taking over farms, and wasn't it a shame they couldn't be let to locals.'

The Thwaites family farmed West Hury, which had a previous existence as the Hare and Hounds public house, but left after ten years to move to High Birk Hatt in 1920. They raised three sons (reduced to two when Leonard died) and two daughters. Life, as John recalls it, was happy if hard, with not much time left over for fun after the daily toil was complete and certainly nothing to spare for luxuries. In Baldersdale, as in all societies, there was a definite upper strata, a small group of families which occasionally demonstrated their comparative affluence.

'Oh yes, the dale had its élite. The Dents were definitely the leaders with the Walkers, the Sayers and the Coulthards close behind. The Dents owned the very first car in Baldersdale and that created quite a stir. I remember being at school when they first drove it round the place and the teacher brought us all out on to the road to have a closer look at this amazing thing. I do not recall what kind it was, but I know that the next car to come into the dale was a bull-nosed Morris and that was owned by the Walkers.

'I cannot recall the dates but it must have been in the very late twenties if I was still at school, because I left just as soon as I could when I made up fourteen. Everybody did in those days. Discipline was very severe at that school, with the cane for the boys and the strap for the girls an everyday thing. There was one teacher who used to get so mad that she would throw slates around, with the whole class ducking out of the way. But that teacher also turned out a lot of good scholars – some even passed the examination for grammar school, although not all those who did actually went. My sister, Violet, was one she coached to that standard but she wasn't able to take her place at grammar school because the uniform she had to have was beyond the means of my family.

'Trouble with that school was the monotony. There was no variety at all – you knew exactly what you would be doing at any given moment of the week. Prayers first thing, then arithmetic, then geography and so on. There were no facilities for sport and we never played football or cricket. Physical training was done in clogs and boots. I couldn't wait to be fourteen and be free of the place. But then I found out just how hard life could really be. I left school one day and was out in the fields muckspreading the next. And it was a seven-day-a-week job from then on.

'But when the young folk of the dale were given a few hours off we certainly made the most of it. There were dances in the Hut by the Strathmore Arms and when we grew up a bit and thought our fathers wouldn't find out we would nip into the Strathmore Arms for a pint, on the few occasions we could afford. It was pretty flat stuff, but we knew no better at the time. Not that you met girls at the Strathmore. It was strictly for males and I do not recall ever seeing a woman in there. She would have been considered trash, the lowest of the low, if one had dared to enter.'

Courtship in Baldersdale had well-defined rules. Romance between the children of established families and hired hands was firmly banned. The inheritance factor was the reason. Marriages were not exactly arranged, but the daughter of a landowning family was expected to wed the son of a family of similar means. The system caused many a broken heart over the generations. The Thwaites obviously did not subscribe to this tradition (after all, they were not even considered Baldersdalians!) since John met his future bride when she was fifteen and in service at a farm in Lunedale. Contrary to the norm for a Yorkshire dale, the young men did venture outside to seek their partners and John met Marie at a fair. Their courtship was conducted as avidly as time and finances would allow. In common with other heads of families in Baldersdale, John's father wasn't overgenerous with either.

'I got two shillings from my dad every Saturday night – that was my week's wages. And I was allowed to go out most weekends. I had a bike and could pedal down to Middleton in Teesdale, meet Marie, take her to the pictures – not the best seats, mind – then buy us both fish and chips and still have change out of that two bob. As it happens, she was much better off than me because her weekly wage was five shillings.

'But there were occasions when it just wasn't possible to get time off to meet her, especially during vital periods such as haymaking. And there was no way of getting a message out to say I couldn't get out, so she would be left hanging about waiting hopefully. But she understood, because she had been brought up on a farm.

'Haytiming, we worked every daylight hour and often into the night. Every blade of grass was needed and we cut everything and anything – dykes, gutters, roadsides, hedgerows – anywhere it grew. One year I had worked nearly a month flat out, every day without a waking hour to myself. Another Saturday came round with no prospect of a night off when it began to rain in the afternoon. Me and my dad were about to cut these dykes when it came on hard. My father stopped, looked at me for a bit and then said that in the circumstances I could go out that night – providing I milked the cows first. All twenty-five of them, and all by hand, of course. By gum, cows have never been milked so fast, never. But it was still ten o'clock before I could get down to meet Marie. And she was still there, waiting for me!'

According to John and Marie, who finally married him and came to Baldersdale when she was twenty, Hannah played no part in the courtship rituals of Baldersdale. Beyond a few exceedingly brief encounters at dances attended by soldiers stationed around

Barnard Castle, she apparently never had a romantic association. There is evidence to suggest that young swains showed interest from time to time but were probably defeated by lack of time and opportunity on the one hand and by Hannah's shy, reserved nature on the other. Her expectations, fed by the romantic figures of literature, were possibly too high and, sadly, Baldersdale was seriously deficient in heroes of the classic mould. But the community did have a couple of heroes in the military sense when the Second World War came, both members of a family which plays a leading role in the modern legends of Baldersdale – the Fawcetts of West Birk Hatt.

Sam Fawcett, who is warmly remembered by Hannah, was by any standards a remarkable man and the head of a remarkable family. Sam sired eight children. At least two of them were big men in every sense of the word. George and Sidney Fawcett were both well over six feet in height, both joined the regular army before war broke out, and both were guardsmen. George joined the Grenadiers and Sidney the Coldstreams. Both saw action of the most extreme kind and both were captured by the Germans. Both escaped from captivity, but only George survived.

To this day, George Fawcett is an imposing man both in stature and personality and lives in a cottage at

Hunderthwaite, the entrance to Baldersdale. He has a wry sense of humour and an uncompromising disposition, particularly when it comes to talking about deeds of valour. Basically, he avoids discussion of his amazing wartime adventures, preferring to indicate that it was all a mistake.

'I didn't want to go into the Army at all,' he will tell you. 'I wanted to go into the Royal Air Force, always did. I wanted to fly – still do. If you got me a microplane right now I would get into it and fly it. I've never been in one but I've read so much about how to do it I'm sure I could manage it.'

And you believe him. George Fawcett may be in his seventies but the will is obviously as strong as ever. To learn about the story of his exploits in enemy territory it is necessary to dig out the cuttings of newspapers printed forty-five years ago. They indicate that the big lad from West Birk Hatt is probably one of the finest unsung heroes of the last war.

The details beggar belief. George kicked off his war by joining the small group of fighting men who courageously volunteered to stay behind and fight a rearguard action in Dieppe in September 1940. He survived but was inevitably captured. Two days of forced marching without food towards a prisoner-of-war camp was too much for this free spirit from

Baldersdale and he escaped. He was on the run for forty-three days, sheltering for part of the time in a cornfield, being fed occasionally by sympathetic French farmers, but was hunted down and sent to captivity in Belgium.

They did not keep him long, however, and this time he made off with a companion and even had the nerve to work for three months on a French farm before starting a marathon trek across the entire length of France. He and his fellow escapee had been told that if they could get to Marseilles, then in unoccupied France, they stood a good chance of finding a ship bound for England. They swam rivers to avoid heavily guarded bridges and doubtless George used the field-craft taught to him by his father Sam to live off the land. They finally reached Marseilles, an enormous distance, particularly when you consider the devious route they must have taken, but were unlucky enough to be spotted by the Vichy French, who were in league with the Nazis. They were led in chains through the streets and dispatched to Italy. George fretted away a whole year there until the Allies landed in Sicily. He was sent in a cattle truck through the Brenner Pass to Austria, where food was so short that he exchanged a piano accordion (the Fawcetts, it seems, were always able to find the means to make music) for two loaves of bread baked from chestnuts. The next year was spent in forced labour in Silesia until the advancing Russian armies precipitated another move, this one the worst of all. George was placed towards the end of a gigantic column, headed by five thousand Jews in poor physical condition. They were marched, often in sub-zero temperatures, through Germany to Czecho-slovakia. The Jews fell in their hundreds and were seen lying dead by the roadside by George and the others as they passed by. He endured six weeks of this ordeal before the chance came to escape once again. The route passed through a wood and George was off like a Baldersdale-bred hare. They never caught him again. He came across a cave where three hundred partisans were quartered and fought side by side with them until the end of the war. On one occasion he played an active role in destroying a German column which yielded twenty-five trucks and three tanks to the partisans. He finished up fighting with the Czech resistance in Prague until the Russians arrived. George went across to introduce himself to the Red Army, an event which boggles the imagination. They, no doubt confused beyond belief, gratefully passed him on to the Americans.

George's long war ended on a high note, partially satisfying his keen urge to fly by winging homewards with the Royal Air Force in the belly of a Lancaster bomber.

Baldersdale was *en fête*, or as near to it as the dale ever came, when Guardsman George Fawcett arrived back somewhat unexpectedly from the war. They threw a party in his honour in the old Hut by the Strathmore Arms, where the revels were halted for one minute's silence in memory of George's brother, Guardsman Sidney Fawcett. About his brother, George will talk . . . and with justifiable pride.

'He was a regular soldier like me, went to the Middle East in 1937 and never came back. He fought with the Eighth Army and was mentioned in dispatches when he shot down a German plane with a machine-gun he had captured from an Italian plane. He mounted it on his vehicle and made it work. Then he was captured at Tobruk and sent to a prisoner-of-war camp in Italy, which was guarded by Germans. But he didn't like being imprisoned any more than me and one night made off across the wire with a pal of his, disposing of a sentry along the way. Trouble was, Sidney decided to go back to get the sentry's rifle, obviously thinking it might come in useful. On the way back again to rejoin his mate he inadvertently walked over some gravel, and the noise alerted the guards. They challenged him and he made a run for it. He was shot in the back.

'They left his body lying where it fell for three days, as a warning to the other prisoners. Then some lads from the Cameron Highlanders were given permission to bury him. He is now lying in a military cemetery near Florence.'

The Fawcetts were a fighting family, although neither George nor Sidney received a medal for valour between them – a clear injustice. Their younger brother, Geoffrey, also distinguished himself, rising to the rank of top sergeant and commanding a tank. And he survived. But there was no military tradition in the family and, despite the fame and glory won by his sons, they were still dwarfed by their father, Sam.

He must have been the best-known and most celebrated inhabitant of Baldersdale – excepting Hannah Hauxwell, of course – within living memory. Hannah herself beams with delight at the mention of his name and there cannot be a past or present resident of the dale who does not become animated when the name of Sam Fawcett is mentioned in conversation. Everyone has a story to tell about him.

Sam was a complete countryman, with a pronounced affinity with nature in all its forms. In a sense, he could charm the birds from the trees, because he adopted and tamed a variety of wildlife. His musical ability – and he was entirely self-taught – enlivened the dale for many a year and even reached the ears of the outside world when he was talent-spotted by the BBC. In 1935 he travelled to Newcastle to spin yarns and perform his music on a popular radio show of the day, an achievement equivalent to an appearance these days on a network television show. Apparently this one and only brush with city life impressed him not at all. It seems he was totally bewildered by the streams of traffic and all the noise and was very glad to get back to rural tranquillity.

Sam's other major talent was, to be frank, on the wrong side of a particular, somewhat dubious aspect of the law. Others would share the view of many country-men, that Sam and his family were merely taking a reasonable share of what the fells and waters surrounding their home offered them. But tiresome authority deems that tickling a trout or two or felling the odd wild duck for the supper table is illegal. Poaching, in fact. And Sam was an exceedingly generous man who would frequently furnish the tables of his neighbours, including the Hauxwells, when they were ill or down on their luck.

His son, Guardsman George, freely admits that the

Fawcetts helped themselves judiciously to the region's edible game.

'We couldn't help ourselves. It was bred in us. And we meant no harm, and did none. But you can be sure that no rabbit died of old age in Baldersdale during our time! My father was so good with his gun that even in the dark he could bring 'em down. Unfortunately, that led to a minor accident involving the property of the Hauxwells which I suspect even Hannah will not know about. Her Great-Uncle Isaac, who lived at Low Birk Hatt, used to keep geese and one night just as the light had faded my dad shot what he thought was a duck flying off Hury Reservoir. But when he went to pick it up he was horrified to discover it was one of Isaac's geese. He decided to say nothing and quietly placed the bird by the gate leading to the Hauxwells' place, with its head tucked in as though asleep.

'They must have found it, because it was gone the day after – probably straight into the oven because it was obvious it had been killed, not just died. But to this day they don't know how.'

The activities of the Fawcett family created much frustration among the local constabulary. They knew only too well what was going on in Baldersdale but Sam and his brood were too wily to be caught and the law could expect no help from other residents. There is one classic tale, still retold with immense delight by older Baldersdalians, about the time a police constable arrived in the dale in hot pursuit of the Fawcetts. A report had been received by his inspector that a discreet cull of the wild ducks on Hury Reservoir was under way. Unwisely, he was heard to proclaim that this time he was sure to catch the Fawcetts red-handed (or, more accurately, up to their fetlocks in feathers). This news was swiftly conveyed to Sam at West Birk Hatt, who decided he would have some fun. Two of his sons were sent down to the reservoir, one at either end. When they spotted the constable stealthily approaching one end, the son at the other would fire his gun. Hury is a very long reservoir. When the perspiring policeman had raced to the spot in full expectation of an arrest, he found no trace of dead ducks or guilty Fawcetts. And as he poked around the undergrowth for hidden poachers, another shot would ring out from the far end of the water. Reinvigorated, he would set off in pursuit . . .

This sport went on for hours, well into the evening. Eventually, exhaustion forced the unfortunate man to abandon the chase. As he departed Baldersdale he was heard to announce with some emphasis that if his superiors were so anxious to catch the phantom poachers of Baldersdale, in future they could (expletive deleted) well do it themselves. He would have no further part in it. The dale rocked with mirth for days as the story went the rounds and will probably be retold for another generation to come. There is no record of any further attempts to hunt the Fawcetts.

The elder Hauxwells themselves were known to join forces with Sam in occasionally exploiting the resources of Hury Reservoir. Hannah's much-loved grandfather, James, the Indian Army veteran with a love of poetry, and Sam developed an unusual method of catching eels. When a sheep died or was slaughtered, they would sometimes pack the entrails into a hessian sack and lower it into the beck leading out of the reservoir just below the Hauxwell property. After a while, the sack would be writhing with eels attracted by the delicacies inside.

Along with the Thwaites at High Birk Hatt the Fawcetts kept a neighbourly eye on the Hauxwells when they were at their most vulnerable. There was a standing arrangement: if no smoke was rising from the chimney of Low Birk Hatt by eleven o'clock in the morning the Fawcetts should come to investigate. One day the fire remained unlit because every member of the Hauxwell family was stricken with flu and unable to move. One of Sam's daughters knocked at the front door until a key landed at her feet, dropped painfully from a bedroom window. She let herself in and ministered to their needs, brewing a pot of tea and lighting a good fire.

Such generosity of spirit, added to their many talents, made the Fawcett family the most popular in Baldersdale. Everyone benefited from knowing them so a spot of poaching was not held against them. Anyway, it was not done for profit. Those were hungry days, and the Fawcetts shared the spoils. Nor would Sam Fawcett have ever upset the balance of nature in the dale because he was a naturalist and a conservationist by inclination. He had a deep knowledge of the habits of all the local wildlife and an uncanny knack of befriending them. He had a tame magpie which, in keeping with tradition, would occasionally steal shiny objects, and a short-eared brown owl which was quartered in his barn and developed a habit of flying at the heads of visitors and knocking off their hats. The most famous and best loved of all Sam's wild pets was a swan which he found one day lying prostrate by the side of Hury Reservoir, too weak even to stand. He carried it home and patiently set about restoring it to full health, hand feeding it for days. The swan became so attached to Sam that it stayed for twelve years. He named it Stegman (a steg is a male goose) and it spent most of the summer on the reservoir but always wintered at West Birk Hatt. It would knock on the door with its beak when it required feeding. In the end it was found mortally wounded near the reservoir, apparently the loser of an argument with a bunch of domestic stegs. The entire dale mourned its passing.

Sam was also a masterly shepherd and an expert breeder of Swaledale sheep, a most hardy animal which roams at will along the high fells and can live through all but the most brutal winters, even possessing the stamina to survive being buried for days under several feet of snow, so long as there is an air hole. The fells around Baldersdale are dangerous places, full of hidden ghylls – deep water holes – and moss bogs which can swallow a man whole. Sam knew every square inch of this territory, sure-footed even on winter nights, and a recognized guide to those who had need to travel the moors. There was no one more adept at tracing and rescuing sheep trapped in snowdrifts.

He could also play a variety of instruments (and passed on this ability to his children) and knew songs and melodies which had never been written down – just passed on from ear to ear via generations of Dalesmen. True folk music.

What a man he must have been. He has fittingly

been given a measure of local immortality by Mrs Lavinia Mary Thwaites, who spent much time in the man's jovial company. Now retired and living in Cotherstone, she still glows at the memory of parties thrown by the Thwaites and the Fawcetts. She is a natural historian who has spent years researching and collecting information about Baldersdale and the surrounding area, delivering lectures to local societies and writing for Teesdale publications. She also possesses poetic talents. Sam Fawcett inspired her to these lines:

The love of the hills has got into your blood,
  The feel of the ling 'neath your feet.
The call of the birds has made it seem good
  As you carefully tended your sheep.
With a bag well stocked with a loving fare,
  Each morning you'd set on your round.
With never a thought, be it near or far, 'ere
  The wandering lost sheep would be found.
And out on the moors so lonely to those
  Who seek the gay lights of the town?
Where curlew and redshank and lapwing repose,
  Great peace and contentment you found.
When the day's work was done and t'was
    Eventide,

The True Daughter of Balder

You'd turn your face homeward and say
To the faithful old dog who walked by your side,
Well, Moses, we've had a most glorious day.

ELEVEN

The 'Heirs' of Hannah

The impact made on the public by Hannah Hauxwell and *Too Long a Winter* has been well
recorded and the lady herself must be on the permanent checklist of every other news editor in the land.
Constant references to Hannah are made in newspapers and her programmes often became a yardstick
by which other documentaries were judged, particularly those made by the Yorkshire Television team
which created it.

Yet *Too Long a Winter* was not entirely devoted to
the story of Hannah Hauxwell. Indeed, she scarcely
figures in the programme until the second half. Most
of the first half was devoted to a remarkable family
called Bainbridge and their love–hate relationship
with a farm called Birkdale, which some consider to
be the biggest agricultural challenge in the Yorkshire
Dales. The farmhouse crouches, as though in permanent search of shelter, in a hollow dominated by fells,
which reach up to two thousand feet, close by where
the counties of Yorkshire, Durham and Westmorland

meet (the bureaucrats would challenge that assertion since they decided, for reasons best known to themselves, to mess around with the old boundaries – but just ask any local).

If you draw a direct line from Low Birk Hatt to Birkdale it would measure less than five miles, so Hannah and the Bainbridges are virtually neighbours. But it is seven miles from Birkdale to the nearest road – seven miles which are difficult enough in the middle of summer and frequently impossible in winter.

The first time Mary Bainbridge saw Birkdale she had emerged from a howling blizzard, having walked the seven miles with one child in her arms, another clinging on to her skirts and a third sitting on a horse-drawn sledge carrying the family furniture. Her husband had set his heart on this savage place when he first saw it as a teenager, working at a now-defunct pyrites mine close to Birkdale, and saw it as a splendid area to raise Swaledale sheep. Mary set about raising the children as Brian's flock multiplied satisfactorily to provide them with a living in their beautiful isolation. They lived happily there for seventeen years until one savage winter practically wiped out their livelihood. Three hundred and fifty sheep perished. Brian's laconic description of this catastrophe yielded the very title of 'Hannah's programme': 'It wasn't starvation that killed them, 'cause food was dropped by heli-copter. It was just too long a winter.'

'Too long a winter' – the phrase leapt from the screen when the rushes were viewed, although within days of transmission – and for ever after at Yorkshire Television – the documentary was referred to simply as 'Hannah'. The Bainbridges, to all intents and pur-poses, sank without trace under the tidal wave of public fascination with Hannah. None of the gifts and ceaseless telephone calls was concerned with them, and out of sackfuls of letters only half a dozen expressed any interest in their story, good though it was. One sequence showed Brian scrabbling with his bare hands deep down into a large drift of snow to locate, and haul to safety, a totally buried sheep. Powerful enough to have excited a fair amount of response from the public under normal circumstances but buried like the sheep under the Hannah Hauxwell avalanche.

All this did not escape the notice of the power-brokers of ITV. Neither did the reviews, which were ecstatic, even from the top, normally hard-to-please critics:

'Beautiful . . . Hannah Hauxwell is Wordsworthian.'
(Nancy Banks-Smith, *Guardian*)

'A marvellous Yorkshire documentary swept by fresh and haunting visual felicities . . . Miss Hannah Hauxwell is a TV natural.'　　　　(Sean Day-Lewis, *Daily Telegraph*)

'Beautifully photographed . . .'

(Peter Black, *Daily Mail*)

'A perfect example of a regional company striking gold in its own back yard.'　(Philip Purser, *Sunday Telegraph*)

'Nothing short of magical . . .'　　　　(*Daily Express*)

'Stark and stunning . . .'　　　　(*Daily Mirror*)

'Hannah Hauxwell, a saint . . .'

(*Telegraph and Argus*, Bradford)

'Astonishing sequences . . .'　　(*Evening News*, London)

And Bob MacAlindin of the *Evening Express*, Aberdeen, who described it as 'a mini classic', made this remarkable declaration:

'Every now and then a television programme transcends the medium which carries it, and out of the technological tube in your living room filters something that strikes at life itself. In this case, it was a person . . . Hannah Hauxwell.'

The 'Heirs' of Hannah

This curious, tattered lady from out of nowhere became the criterion, the very touchstone for the *Too Long a Winter* production team, which was to stay together for more than a decade. She had transcended all the barriers of language and class. She was both universal and unique. There was no point in looking for more Hannahs. The task was, rather, to seek the essence of Hannah . . . to find people and situations which, however simple and unremarkable by accepted standards, nevertheless projected the eternal verities which humans in whatever condition could recognize instantly and then identify with.

That was the discipline the team obeyed as it went out to try and find the subjects to perpetuate this fragile, golden thread.

The heirs of Hannah Hauxwell came quickly to the ITV network screen.

The first successor was *Children of Eskdale*, about the Raw family living a glorious life in a superb farm on the North Yorkshire moors with their five bonny kids. The storyline was simple – Dad wanted a tractor, the kids wanted a pony. The final sequence moved all those who watched it as John Raw secretly bought Prince, the pony he knew the children were besotted with, and quietly tethered it in the back pasture. Then he sent his eldest son, ten-year-old Alan Raw, out on a spurious errand. Hidden cameras recorded the reaction of the children as they poured out of the back door to greet Prince, still only half believing it was really meant for them. It wasn't just their mother, Dot Raw, who cried at the sight of the pure joy of the children. To the somewhat less innocent joy of Yorkshire Television, this was also rapturously received by the public and critics alike. Nancy Banks-Smith, the finest essayist in Fleet Street, who could decorously lacerate a programme whilst ostensibly writing about the contents of her grandmother's handbag, ended her review with a declaration –

'A classic', she wrote.

Then came *Sunley's Daughter*, a love story set in the same stretch of high moorland along the banks of the Esk. This, and *The Dale that Died*, a stirring story from Upper Wensleydale, *A Chance in Life*, and others, were all received in a manner which stunned the production team. Although some were far from classics – indeed, one or two were fairly ordinary – the pattern was repeated every time the same team brought a programme to the screen. Enormous Press attention before and after transmission became standard (and led directly to large audiences), and the ghost of 'Saint' Hannah loomed over them all. Scarcely a newspaper piece about this new wave of documentaries, stretching over several years, failed to include a reference to the revered inhabitant of Low Birk Hatt Farm.

International attention, sales and acclaim followed swiftly, and so did the awards and honours. The most coveted in the world is the Prix Italia, and when a jury of twelve top television executives met to pick the British entry for 1974, six votes were cast for *Too Long a Winter* and five for *Children of Eskdale*. A single vote went to one of the batch of other nominees. So, 'Hannah' – the documentary, not the lady – went to Florence flying the Union Jack, and *Children of Eskdale* was granted an 'Honours Night', shown before a packed and extraordinarily appreciative audience on the giant screen at a Florentine cinema.

Too Long a Winter was also applauded after its showing in competition, the only film accorded that spontaneous honour – and was the very clear favourite to win the trophy. Unfortunately, it failed. There is a bitter theory about the reason. A worthy, if pedestrian, documentary from Japan was selected, a decision which even rendered the Japanese speechless. An Italian gentleman, exuding both importance and anger, approached the disconsolate Yorkshire Television contingent and said, 'Gentlemen, if you enter your marvellous film for the Trento Festival, I am sure it will win. Let me have a copy.' He was right. 'Hannah' went on to be honoured in New York in the Emmy

Awards and ended with a clutch of *objets d'art* for the boardroom.

'Hannah' and her heirs played a leading role in establishing a documentary department which became internationally recognized for its standards of excellence.

POSTSCRIPT

There is a season in the life of Hannah Hauxwell which has for years been urgently desired by those who care for her welfare. To retire . . . to leave Low Birk Hatt, to put behind her the punishing burden of running a farm totally unaided.

A small group of constant friends have watched, pleaded, waited and despaired as she turned their attempts at persuasion aside with typical courtesy and gentle phrases and then carried on, her physical condition visibly deteriorating, fighting a gradually losing battle with Low Birk Hatt, where every midwinter is deep. It was frighteningly clear that each passing year sapped a little more of her remaining reserves of strength.

Her situation was precarious enough during her pre-television days when every penny had to be watched and she could only afford to keep one cow and its calf. The material benefits which come automatically with fame did not, regretfully, improve Hannah's daily regime on the farm. Indeed, they led directly to a significant increase in her workload as she invested in more cattle. Friends who waded thigh-deep through the drifts in January and February were horrified to find her painfully dragging loads of fodder on a sledge over the snow to feed this vastly expanded family (all fondly given a pet name). The sound of her rasping breath as she heaved herself and heavy bales over stone walls could be heard across two meadows.

All this led inevitably to a serious decline in the state of her living quarters. As Hannah herself is fond of saying, she has to be both the farmer and the farmer's wife. So the time available to attend to household duties such as cleaning, dusting and washing, etc. was dramatically depleted. Her cherished beasties came first . . . and second and third.

To be frank, Hannah's living conditions degenerated into a sorry mess. A dwelling once capable of housing seven people became so crowded with various objects, including parcels from all round the world (some of which appeared to be unopened), that movement was severely restricted. Hannah clings firmly on to things which are eminently disposable, such as bits of string, plastic bags and containers, brown paper, even empty beans tins. To throw anything away constituted an unforgivable waste, a state of mind doubtless conditioned by the memory of those early days when poverty, even the threat of malnutrition, was a very real factor. The situation became so bad that corridors had to be created through this confusion of items, so narrow that two people found it difficult to pass.

Cobwebs draped the ceiling and walls, dust lay thickly on most surfaces and wallpaper fell limply from the walls. Most rooms were colonized during the winter by mice – and rats. Rats are deadly. You can die from food polluted by rats, or even by placing your hand where one has urinated. Naturally, this created another major worry for those concerned about Hannah's safety.

Dimly perceptible through this spectacular untidiness, however, was the superb basic quality of a great deal of the furniture. One or more of Hannah's forebears must have possessed both good taste and the money to go with it, because they brought to Low Birk Hatt wardrobes and chests of drawers constructed in oak and mahogany by craftsmen of the old school. There were also case clocks, organs, four-poster beds ornately carved, and much more; some a touch worm-eaten, but most well over a century old and clearly valuable as antiques.

All in all, Hannah was the sole owner of possessions which – if only she would sell up and escape – would yield enough capital to keep her in comfort. For, even if she sold her land and buildings at the lower end of a conservative valuation, there would be enough to buy a desirable dwelling in one of the villages near Baldersdale, with sufficient in hand to invest and supplement her pension.

So there was a measure of cautious rejoicing when, at the beginning of 1988, Hannah yielded in small measure to all those years of gentle persuasion by at least agreeing to look at properties on the books of Teesdale estate agents. Just to look, mind you . . . no commitment.

Then, in the spring of that year, she was attracted by a cottage on sale in Mickleton. It answered all the complex requirements outlined by Hannah when she described the type of property which may – just may, mind – incline her towards leaving Low Birk Hatt. The cottage in question had two and a half acres of pastureland which meant she could take Rosa, the senior cow, along with her. She would even have room for a few hens and a goat. The place was detached and had some very useful outbuildings, including a stone-built stable just right for Rosa's winter quarters. Such matters were clearly as important as the two bedrooms, lounge, dining room, kitchen and utility room and the luxury of water on tap.

The cottage was due to be publicly auctioned at the King's Head Hotel, Barnard Castle, and Hannah agonized for a week over the top price she would bid. Not that she would attend the auction in person – that would be no place for a maiden lady of delicate disposition. A group of eager friends, delighted at the momentous decision, agreed to represent her. One of them, a man experienced in the local property market and who had wide knowledge of the pitfalls, was selected to do the bidding. It became clear that Hannah had set her heart on this property as, over the last four days before the auction, she raised her top offer every day. As the party departed for the King's Head she whispered into the ear of a confidante that another five hundred pounds could be added, if it became absolutely necessary.

But for an unfortunate quirk of fate, the property would now be Hannah's new home. Her final bid was sufficient to beat all local opposition, but a couple said to be moving back to Teesdale after a spell in the London area were obviously prepared to go much higher than the expected price. It was assumed they considered the cottage, knocked down at £36,000, to be rather cheap when compared with south-eastern prices. They and Hannah were the last two bidders.

Hannah accepted the bad news philosophically. The friends seemed to register more distress, because they realized that through sheer bad luck a very rare opportunity had been missed.

As the summer of 1988 slipped damply and miserably away, the gloom of the Hannah Hauxwell

Supporters' Club deepened perceptibly. There were no further signals from Low Birk Hatt that the lady was contemplating any other property. There was, however, one very ominous signal from another quarter – that the winter of 1988/9 could be a really bad one.

'We're due one . . . all the signs are there,' said local opinion. The potential accuracy of this sombre forecast was reinforced in autumn when the temperature dipped below zero and snow-ploughs churned through to keep the roads of Baldersdale open.

If there was to be a repeat of the 1978/9 agony, when the power failed, her clothes became sheet ice on her back and the sole source of warm nourishment was Rosa's milk, there would be serious doubts about Hannah's ability to survive.

For heaven's sake, apart from everything else, she suffers from angina . . .

Then it happened – and no one is quite sure how or when she made her decision. Frankly, her friends had run out of variations on the old theme of the desperate urgency to get out of Low Birk Hatt and were directing their energies towards plans to cope with the emergencies to come. But, quite unexpectedly, she announced her intention to bid for a cottage in Cotherstone, recently placed on the market. There was to be no auction this time, just the usual private negotiation through an estate agent.

Belle Vue Cottage is ideally suited to Hannah's needs, situated in the middle of an attractive Dales village. There is a combined post office and shop which sells the famous Cotherstone cheese, another shop with petrol pumps, two pubs (not that Hannah will have much need of them) and a friendly population – and readily available medical facilities.

Negotiations for the property went like a dream. The lively octogenarian who owned Belle Vue Cottage (and was moving further north to be near her relatives) turned out to be one of the vast army of Hannah 'fans'. She was so delighted that her meticulously maintained and cherished home was favoured by Hannah that she attempted to drop the price (and this in an area where property had recently been known to attract bids over and above the asking price). It is safe to assume that anyone else interested was not encouraged. When the sale was agreed, the news spread like a moorland grass fire throughout Cotherstone. Hannah was coming to live there! Delight was widespread, particularly among some ladies who once lived themselves in Baldersdale and knew Hannah from the old days. However, it was nothing compared to the monumental relief felt by the people who had worked towards this for more years than they cared to recall.

A support team moved into action immediately. It was led by Kathy Rooney (who was helping to produce the latest television documentary) and Richard Megson (who runs the youth hostel in Baldersdale and has long been the selfless helper on the spot). Mightily did they labour. Day by day they guided Hannah through the valuation and sale of her property, organizing estate agents, solicitors, bank managers, removal companies and getting to personal grips with the huge task of clearing out the amazing contents of Low Birk Hatt (a glance at the photograph in this book of Hannah sitting among her belongings will convey the scene better than the proverbial thousand words).

It went on for weeks, complicated as it was by Hannah's innate reluctance, born of earlier deprivation, to throw anything away on the grounds that 'one never knows when it might come in useful'. Many items of dubious value were retained for later dispatch to Cotherstone, but eventually the night sky of Baldersdale was illuminated by the flames of a large bonfire built from several decades of rubbish.

As one would expect, a crisis developed over the beloved beasts. There was no room for Rosa at Belle Vue Cottage, and the thought of the senior cow and all her progeny going to goodness knows what fate at the auction mart was totally unacceptable. A loyal friend and neighbour, Bill Purves of Clove Lodge, agreed to take them on and assured Hannah that he would care for them as she would wish.

The final parting was not a happy time. Those who witnessed it were visibly affected themselves as Hannah bade farewell one misty afternoon. She watched them disappear through the iron gate and down the new road, her face white and wet with distress.

Hannah took most of her best furniture to Cotherstone, and there was precious little to put into the farm sale since Low Birk Hatt boasted none of the modern equipment other farms possess. Some stone troughs, a few scythes and rakes, a quantity of horse-drawn equipment, but not much else. Nevertheless, more than two hundred people (plus film crews, reporters and photographers) trudged through the glutinous mud to be there, and Clifford Pratt, an archetypal Dales auctioneer from Hawes in Upper Wensleydale, conducted the sale with gravelly skill. His understated, classic Northern humour helped to spur occasional spirited bidding. Some of the four-poster beds, tables and other antique pieces which would not fit into Belle Vue Cottage yielded useful sums and the overall sale result exceeded expectations.

The sealed bids for the farmhouse and land were equally satisfactory. The one which caused deepest pleasure in Hannah was from a conservation organization which had spotted that one particular parcel of her land was so unspoiled and unpolluted by artificial fertilizers that it was virtually unique for miles around, a haven for rare grasses and wild flowers.

This land will be kept in exactly the way Hannah kept it, the way her ancestors kept it for centuries, and it will be named after her.

Hannah is too private a person to disclose publicly the sum she accepted for her property, but after paying in full for her new home and all expenses it seems certain that her future is secure – financially, at least. A revolutionary concept when compared to the years she spent living well below the lowest of subsistence levels.

Now . . . it all sounds like a happy ending fashioned by a romantic novelist. But a very real trauma remains. All those who stayed by her side during this latest season in the remarkable life of Hannah Bayles Tallentire Hauxwell know it.

They saw her sitting in the one remaining chair in a house hollow with emptiness after the farm sale, so deep in an unspoken grief that everyone and everything else could have been a thousand miles away.

They saw her in the cab of the removal van as it was dragged by tractor out of the snow and ice of Baldersdale, clutching her dog, Timmy, and staring with unseeing eyes at the spectacular sunset gilding the shimmering waters of the Mississippi, her name for the sinuous reservoir over which Low Birk Hatt perches.

There is central heating, a flush toilet, hot running water and – Lord help us! – an ex-directory telephone awaiting her in Cotherstone.

But as the winter of 1988/9 closed in, there was no doubt where the heart of Hannah is lodged, now and possibly for ever:

Low Birk Hatt, Baldersdale.

'Wherever I go . . . and whatever I am . . .
this is me . . .'

ACKNOWLEDGEMENT

This book was largely based on
taped conversations with Hannah
Hauxwell, principally conducted
by Kathy Rooney, to whom
Hannah and Barry Cockcroft
express profound gratitude.

Barry Cockcroft also extends thanks to
former residents of Baldersdale who so
generously assisted with their
recollections and photographs of times
past, particularly John and Marie Thwaites,
the Fawcett family and Lavinia Thwaites.